Our Neighbors, Their Voices

True Stories of Immigrant Exodus

Jordan Steven Sher

D1314509

Front cover picture: Pina (front), Marisa (left), Mamma (middle), Luciana (right) circa 1961

This book in independently published by Kindle Direct Publishing, a division of Amazon

Publisher: Independently published (May 28, 2019)
Language: English
Copyright@2019

Some of the people I interviewed preferred anonymity for themselves, their families, and the places they lived, so I have honored that request by using pseudonyms

"I learned that courage was not the absence of fear, but the triumph over it. The brave man is not he who does not feel afraid, but he who conquers that fear."

Nelson Mandela

Contents

Prologue

What are you? If I asked you this, would you say just "I'm American"? Or would you know the ethnic roots of your parents, grandparents, and even more distant ancestors? What about your neighbors, colleagues, or folks you pass on the street — do you know their stories? If they look or sound different than you, do you avoid interacting with them?

We are in a tough place in this country today. Immigrants are and have been the "heart and soul" of this nation since its inception — indeed, since long before it was a nation. Still, for every wave of immigrants over the decades and centuries, there has been prejudice, stereotypes, bigotry, and hate from those who perceive the newcomers as a threat.

I've always found this curious, because immigrants have been coming to this country for many thousands of years. The first human beings to arrive on this continent — 20,000 years ago or even earlier, according to archeological and DNA evidence — most likely traveled from Asia via an ancient land bridge to present-day Alaska. How they made their way southward and, ultimately, populated the entire Northern, Central, and Southern Americas is still being debated. Nonetheless, they were the original newcomers to this land.

It was not until the late eleventh century, and more prodigiously in the fourteenth and early fifteenth centuries, that Europeans found their way to North America. They brought soldiers, disease, greed, and fear to the native population, and reduced their numbers. As America established itself, its military corralled the native people into reservations and took over much of their land.

In the early seventeenth century, the French and the English came to this country for two purposes: to expand their wealth and power in the New World, and to practice their religion freely. The notion that this new land offered vast opportunity on many fronts began to proliferate.

As such, the plantations of the South required labor to work the crops. The economy depended on this new system (at least new to this country) of slavery. Africans were taken from their homes against their will to build profit for their "owners," and the idea of people as property took shape. Racism took hold as a result of many factors, and its prejudice and violence remain woven in the fabric of our society.

Still, America was viewed as a "land of opportunity" for many, and as a place of freedom for most who immigrated here in waves during the nineteenth and twentieth centuries. Whether it was the Irish fleeing famine, or the Italians fleeing poverty, or the Jews escaping anti-Semitism in the form of pogroms in Eastern Europe or Nazi genocide, or other Europeans coming for economic opportunity, or Southeast Asians fleeing war-torn communities, or Chinese seeking work, or Bosnian-Muslims fleeing genocide, or Latin Americans seeking economic salvation, or anyone else in pursuit of freedom from tyranny, the United States has always been that "beacon of light."

That "light" has not always shone so brightly. As early as 1798, when America was preparing for war with France, the second president of the United States, John Adams, had signed into law the Alien and Sedition Acts, which gave broad powers to the government to deport foreigners and to make it harder for new immigrants to vote. Fear and anger toward these people spread, and many were at risk of being jailed or deported.

In the early 1940s, as war with Japan roared to life, many Japanese and Japanese-Americans were interned in concentration camps throughout the western United States. This policy was even upheld by the U.S. Supreme Court as necessary to protect the safety and security of our country. In 1988, President Ronald Reagan signed the Civil Liberties Act, which offered a formal apology and monetary compensation for this appalling time in our history.

After the tragedy of September 11, 2001, when terrorists destroyed the World Trade Center and damaged the Pentagon, killing almost 3,000 people, Islamophobia took hold in this country and worldwide. This has created fear and prejudice against Muslims, even as many of them are refugees, fleeing horrific conditions in various parts of the Middle East.

Our country is now at a crossroads. Are we a humane society adhering to the tenets of "give us your tired, your poor, your hungry," or are we putting up walls both literally and figuratively? We must determine whether we can no longer afford to be what we have represented to the world, or whether we must find a way to continue to do so.

I want to share the stories of immigrants today who, as in past waves, have left their countries of origin. Often, they were driven out by fear, political repression, war, or crime. Are there criminals who have entered our country? Of course. Did some streets of New York become inhabited with gangs of Irish men who came after the potato famine to engage in criminal activities? Yes. Did some Italian immigrants enter organized crime? Sure.

The majority, however, were seeking a better life. That is the nature of immigration at its heart. Without them, our country would be bland and less advanced, to be sure. Today, think of the technology entrepreneur Elon Musk, who grew up in South Africa, or the cellist YoYo Ma, who was born in France but is of Chinese descent. They are some of the extraordinary individuals who have contributed to our lives. Yet it is the everyday person, the immigrant whose name you don't know, the one who has in many small ways touched the lives of so many — these are the people from whom this book draws its lifeblood. These are the people who, if they had not been welcomed, would be missed in the multicultural landscape that is America. These are our neighbors, and here are their voices.

A Lawyer's Unique Perspective

By Lucy Lee, Attorney-at-Law
Fallon, Bixby, Cheng & Lee, Inc.,

I am the daughter of immigrants. My parents and grandparents left China after World War II to escape persecution from the Communists. My maternal grandmother did not escape China and she died during the Cultural Revolution. She was accused of being a Counter-Revolutionary Capitalist for having food to give away during World War II to her fellow villagers to save them from starvation.

My family came with very little money and could not speak English. They worked hard, doing low paying jobs – they took work as farmers, truck drivers, cooks, and seamstresses. They did not make much money, but they learned to save, and to encourage me and my four sisters and brother to learn English and do well in school because that would shape our future in America.

My parents eventually took a risk and opened their own business, a restaurant in San Francisco. For about fourteen years I worked for them. I spent every moment after school, and on weekends in the restaurant. I studied when customers were not around, and after work. Often, I worked 60 to 80 hours a week depending on when I took turns with my sisters to attend school. I learned to wait on tables, clean, do the accounting, and cook. I can still de-vein three pounds of shrimp in less than five minutes!

To illustrate that my family had become Americanized, we served Chinese food, but we also served hamburgers with french fries and milkshakes. The most important values I learned were how to deal effectively and courteously with people that hard work is a good thing, and that family always comes first.

I worked in the restaurant until the time I became an immigration lawyer. I have worked for small as well as very large law firms since then. About twenty years ago, I took ownership of, and became managing attorney with the oldest immigration law firm in San Francisco.

For me this work is more than just practicing law. While I truly feel joy helping people obtain work visas, permanent residence, citizenship, and uniting families, this work is personal. It has emanated from what my parents wanted for their family, and the values they instilled in us. Through this work I can enable others to have an opportunity to love this country as much as I do.

Immigrating to America is often a long and sometimes difficult path for many. Some people are sponsored by employers for their skilled work talents. Some people are sponsored by family members. Some risk death to reach the United States. Regardless of the path, everyone has to overcome many shared obstacles. Immigrants must be able to sustain a living here, and contribute to our country in some way. It is no mystery that feeling secure in this country as an immigrant is no easy feat. Many face the obstacles before them, not speaking English. Most immigrants want to retain their cultural backgrounds, but also be a part of the American tapestry. I have seen firsthand the resilience, perseverance, and fortitude with which they push forward, and I applaud them.

It is a special status and an honor to be an immigrant in America. Only about a tenth of the people in the United States are foreign born while everyone else is a descendent of immigrants. Immigrants, who might not bring much with them materially to this country, do bring a mighty work ethic. They also bring a sense of optimism and the belief that tomorrow will be brighter than today. For example, over the past couple of decades, immigrant engineers have started hundreds of technology businesses in Silicon Valley. These new immigrant entrepreneurs created jobs, exports, and wealth for our region. At the same time, they have accelerated the integration of California into the global economy.

Over the course of my twenty-seven years as an immigration attorney, I have worked with immigrants of all socio-economic and religious backgrounds, from all over the world. While I have clients in the high-tech industry, I have also worked with people who are teachers, dancers and monks. Some clients flee their home countries seeking asylum based on their political or religious beliefs, or for their sexual orientation. Families are sometimes separated for years due to either the complexity of their kin relationship, or quota backlogs.

Irrespective of the classification of how people immigrate to America, a common thread I have long ago realized is that the political, economic, and social climate of our country has a direct impact on immigration law, and that immigrants, being the newcomers, have the least amount of power. Often, they are scapegoated, or used as political pawns.

I always encourage immigrants to naturalize and become United States citizens, so that they can enjoy many privileges and exercise their hard-earned rights. Citizens have the right to vote in our elections and to get involved in what they believe in. As citizens, they can help America face challenges domestically and internationally.

Emerging trends in immigration law fluctuate depending on who is in political power in the United States. For instance, under the Trump Administration, I have seen a great shift from family unification toward decreasing or halting "chain migration," the current negative term to keep loved ones together. Even the most educated and law-abiding individuals are questioned as to why a bachelor's degree is required to undertake certain professions including that of engineers, accountants, and graphic designers. Advanced degrees are no less questioned. Very long government processing times on virtually all case types has become a method to dissuade employers, investors, and individuals from seeking visas, green cards and citizenship.

Despite the difficulties that are imposed upon immigrants, I am grateful that America is still a country built on laws that were created by people who were immigrants themselves, and that overcoming adversity is still possible in the United States.

In 1979, the Ayatollah Ruhollah Khomeini led the revolution that changed Iran from a secular to an Islamic state. Since then, the government has been subject to Sharia (or Islamic) Law, which is derived from the religious teachings of the Koran. Although a president is elected to office (which is not a fair and free election, however), the chief cleric holds the ultimate power in Iran. Despite the fact that many of its citizens want democratic reforms, such changes have rarely been enacted. Most activities that mimic Western values are done in secret and at one's own risk of harassment, arrest, and interrogation or prison.

Dorri

"I am so sad that you are leaving us, habibi, but the oppression that we are living under is too much for a young woman to endure," Dorri's father said as she was preparing to leave her home.

In August 2012, at the age of 23, Dorri was heading to Florida Atlantic University in Boca Raton on a student visa to get a master's degree in biomedical sciences.

Born in Teheran, she was raised in a non-practicing Muslim family. They believed that being a good person and caring for others did not require specific religious teachings. Her friends had no connection to Islam, either.

In many ways, she could have been a typical American girl. As a teenager, she went to friends' parties, enjoyed sharing time with family, and loved school.

But this was not America.

"My parents were always supportive of my goals. We did not practice Islam, and I always felt free to express myself within the confines of my family and circle of friends," she says.

With an interest in science, Dorri knew that she could never pursue her dreams in a country that did not allow freedom, especially for women, to seek the opportunities that their skills and talents could fulfill.

In 2009, there had been unrest on the streets of Teheran. The demonstrators were mostly peaceful. The police were not.

"I am in some way at fault for what this country has come to," Dorri recalls her father saying.

"Why do you say this, Dad?" asked Dorri.

"I was part of the many groups that protested the Shah to bring about democratic changes, but we weren't strong enough, so the religious zealots won out."

The results of Islamic rule have been hard for many in Iran, especially in Teheran.

Dorri had to wear a hijab, a head scarf, and could not express her opinions about the ruling clerics or other matters of state that she disagreed with. Talking politics was unwise if you did not adhere to Sharia Law.

You could not say anything negative about Islam. You could be punished with death by hanging if you did so.

"I was going to an English class once wearing the required black garb, and hijab," Dorri says. "A big, dark van stopped in front of me and a woman got out, as did her colleague with a gun. I was arrested because my hijab was too loose."

While at the police station, she was treated like a criminal. Her crime: not adhering to proper wearing of hijab. Her interrogators subjected her to belittling comments, such as "You are nothing; you are a disgrace to Iran!"

They also took mug shots of her, including a criminal identification number, and threatened her with serious punishment should she be arrested for the same crime again. It was a surreal and frightening experience, she recalls.

Her father went to the police station to sign a statement that she would never wear the hijab in such a way as to insult Islam. He was very angry at the police, and Dorri had to implore him to calm down or they would both be put in jail.

"What is viewed as a normal part of the freedom we have in the U.S. [was] not so in Iran," Dorri says.

For example, secret clubs existed in Iran so that young people could party. They had to remain quiet and be discreet about their alcohol use. If the police learned of these clubs, or even just of parties, they could arrest you, bring you down to the station, and whip or beat you. A common way to avoid being arrested was to pay off the police. Still, sometimes that was not enough, and the consequences could be harsh. This applied to weddings, as well. Most celebrations involved alcohol and dancing. Here, too, the police could pay a visit and look for a pay-off.

"Most of the people, especially in Teheran, are not religious. The government requires them to be deeply invested in Islam, so we have to act as though we are."

"I came to the U.S. while [Mahmoud] Ahmadinejad ruled as president of Iran," says Dorri.

His party, the Society of the Devotees of the Islamic Revolution, closely followed the tenets of the clerics who actually ruled the country. While in power, from 2005 to 2013, he used his influence to impose greater repression than had been previously felt by its citizens.

She describes how horrible he was. "It was he who established the religious police and diminished our freedoms. Those many of us who were secular had to look over our shoulders constantly. At any moment we could be accused of doing something non-Muslim and be at risk for whatever consequences the police would impart. It was a terribly unsafe environment, and we suffered emotionally, as well."

The president before him, Mohammad Khatami, had been a reformer. Dorri says that the country was moving forward under his presidency. He had wanted to bring all Iranians into the political process, but he was too weak to challenge the established hard-liners who controlled key institutions. He remained in office from 1997 to 2005, when the populist Ahmadinejad became president and whose reforms reversed whatever progress was being sought by Khatami. Ahmadinejad's second term in office, after an election that was seen as fraudulent and quite disheartening by most educated Iranians, saw the further erosion of freedom desired by many.

"This was a low point in my life," she explains. "Protests, which my father participated in because of the guilt he felt having been part of the failed movement to bring in democracy, but that ushered in Sharia Law, propelled him to speak out against the madness that had taken hold in our country."

Her arrest by the religious police for wearing her hijab improperly began the process of her thinking about leaving Iran.

"Anytime I wanted to go out, I was so stressed. If I was arrested [again], it would be worse." So, she stayed at home.

There was also another important aspect of Dorri's life that led her to emigrate.

She had experienced pain in her knee for years, and, when she turned 20, a mass in her knee was found and diagnosed as bone sarcoma. Her doctor gave her two weeks to live. Her parents were beside themselves. She had never seen her father cry, but for those weeks he cried often. Fortunately, they sought a second opinion, and the other doctor gave them a more treatable diagnosis of bone lymphoma. Dorri went through chemo, radiation, and other therapies to treat it (and has been in remission ever since). However, the doctor told her that the continued stress she was feeling would only contribute to the risk of relapse.

Her father, who never wished for her to leave the country, reversed his opposition. Her mother, a former teacher, agreed.

"You need to go. You need to take care of yourself," she remembers them saying.

This is when she decided to go to a university in the United States. She had family friends in Boca Raton, Florida, and the only school she applied to was Florida Atlantic University for her master's.

First, though, she needed a visa. This raised some serious concerns. If she applied for asylum in the United States, she would never be allowed to return to Iran or see her family again. Or, if she were forced to return to Iran, then she would be a "marked" woman because she had chosen to leave in the first place —

which would make it dangerous for her to go back to Iran. Ultimately, because she was coming in during the Obama administration, she was able to get a student visa without much delay.

When she got to Florida, she thought she would experience culture shock. She did not.

"When I arrived in Boca, the people were so nice. They smiled at me, not like in Teheran," she says.

"I felt free. The air was fresh, and wonderfully rushed through my hair, with no hijab!"

After her degree training, she found a job at a biotech company in the San Francisco Bay Area in 2016, and she now has an H-1B visa.

Dorri is applying to graduate schools for her Ph.D. The opportunity she has ahead of her in this country is what she had hoped for, despite her longing for her family and for her country. The freedom she feels to express herself, and to be herself, is something that she cherishes.

She also told another story that illustrates the struggle of people wanting to enter this country during the Trump presidency.

An Iranian friend of hers married an American man, and they both went to Napa to celebrate their one-year anniversary. Their car was hit by a drunk driver, and the husband was killed. Dorri's friend was severely injured. The friend's parents flew from Iran to Canada, hoping that they could convince customs to let them visit their daughter in the hospital. But they were refused entry into the United States.

Dorri is sad when telling this story. She loves this new country of hers. She worries about what will happen to people who are here now from other countries. The news stories she reads are disheartening. The difficulties that people have in their former countries often necessitate them leaving. The challenges that are now imposed upon those who arrive can be mind-boggling.

"There is no reason to leave one's country unless faced with some sort of trauma. I had to leave. I love being free. If I was ever forced to leave here, I would still not return to Iran. I would go to Canada or Australia. I have found a life that I would never have had in Iran. I am thankful to live the life I am living now. I will never give it up."

With a population today of only 6.2 million, and having gained its independence from France in 1943, Lebanon has experienced a great deal of turmoil. Situated on the eastern end of the Mediterranean Sea between Israel and Syria, this tiny nation's history has been dominated by assassinations, rapid government changes, wars, occupation by foreign invaders, riots, political instability, the establishment of Hezbollah as the predominant military wing of the government, and the taking in of thousands of Syrian refugees. Tensions between Christians, Shia and Sunni Muslims, Druze, and other, less populated religions have complicated the otherwise rich tapestry of those who inhabit this land.

Walid

Upon meeting Walid, it is difficult to surmise the depth of trauma he experienced in his native country of Lebanon. What surfaces is the resilience: this is a man whose unmistakably positive outlook on life was born out of the fear, tragedy, and courage that consumed much of his time in Tyr, his hometown, and Beirut, the capital of Lebanon.

Tyr, a small city near the Mediterranean Sea, was home to Walid and his family. His paternal grandfather, Ahmad, was a produce merchant in the 1950s who would take the long train trip to Haifa in

Israel to sell his wares. He died in 1986, two years before Walid was born. His great grandfather was a carpenter who helped to build boats used by the fishermen of Tyr; fishing was the primary industry of the city back then.

His maternal grandfather, Abo Yousef, lived in Deir Kanoon, where he owned citrus groves. He was a prestigious man in town: it was he who would settle disputes, like a mediator. His home was always open, so that people would come in, sip tea, and ask for his help.

Walid's father, Nazih, was born in 1951. He had land by the beach and a restaurant, which he opened in 1989 as a small shack and then expanded into a larger establishment. He also worked for the government social security office. He would work there until 1:00 and then go to the restaurant. He is now retired from the government job but still owns the restaurant. Walid attributes his work ethic to his father.

His mother, Nohad, stayed at home to raise the children. His three older sisters, Dima, Tala, and Safiya, now live in Lebanon, Nigeria, and Northern California, respectively. His father's brother also lives in Northern California, and, in 1988, nearing the birth of her son Walid, his mother journeyed to her brother-in-law's home. It was there, in a local hospital, that Walid was born, giving him U.S. citizenship. His mother's decision would foreshadow the path that would eventually lead him to America. (At the time, it was much easier to get U.S. citizenship if one had a close relative living here. Because Walid's uncle lived in California, this allowed him to become a citizen, which opened up the door for his mother, which in turn paved the way for Walid and his sisters.)

Life in Lebanon was good in his early years, despite the threat of war with Israel that seemed to hover over Walid and his family. He had close family ties and lots of friends, and he met many interesting and diverse people while helping out at his father's restaurant. There are many Roman ruins in Tyr that attract tourists, so Walid would meet them, as well. He attributes his understanding and interest in other cultures and people to his early development in Tyr.

Schooling in Lebanon was very strict. The teachers would hit students on the backs of their hands if they were not meeting behavioral or academic expectations. Walid's father, who was prominent in town, informed the principal that his son was not to be punished by the teachers. Walid said some resentment by other students did surface, but he understood this. Still, he says, "I was a good kid anyway, and never got into any trouble."

School was difficult due to the heavy academic expectations. It was there that he learned English, and he attributes this to his proficiency in the language to this day.

His parents are Muslim: his father is Sunni, and his mother is Shia. This never presented any conflict when he was young, Walid says; there were no issues regarding the sects. This may be specific to Lebanon, he says, but until later in his life, this difference did not breed animosity.

Walid chose to be Shia. He sees the Shia as not supporting violence; the Koran teaches peace and cannot be twisted to create violence as a justification for one's fervent beliefs. He is not particularly religious, but he celebrates some holy days with family (the sister and niece with whom he now lives in California).

He tracks his first memories of conflict in his country back to the age of five.

"We used to have incidents that could present a situation where we might have to flee. We had our bags packed just in case."

"In 1993, rockets were shot by Palestinians in Lebanon at Israel. Israelis responded by sending jet fighters into Lebanon. We lived on the fifth floor, and we raced down from our apartment to the emergency shelter underneath our building. I was not afraid for myself, actually, but I was mostly scared for my sisters, especially the youngest one, who was greatly affected by this."

He vividly remembers 1996. He was lying in bed early one morning when his neighborhood seemed to erupt. He first heard anti-aircraft fire coming from a Lebanese tank stationed very close to his apartment. He heard a huge explosion shortly thereafter. An Israeli helicopter had destroyed the tank, rocking his apartment building. Bewildered and frightened, he raced into his parents' bedroom. His parents were panicked, too. With the explosion nearby, his curiosity at first guided him toward the window, but his parents yelled at him to stay away in case ensuing explosions shattered the glass that could have cut him or worse.

"We were all crying and frantic. My parents grabbed us and we headed to the shelter. I was scared, but, once again, more for my sisters. I felt like even as a boy it was my responsibility to make sure that they were safe."

"My parents insisted on leaving Tyr. Our neighbors were in shock and were maybe in denial or just not able to comprehend what was going on, so many remained. We headed up the coast in my father's car, which he was driving like crazy," according to Walid, "to a town called Sidon, between Tyr and Beirut, which we believed was safer as there was no military value there, and Hezbollah was far from there. To our left, in the Mediterranean, were Israeli gun boats firing rockets overhead. I couldn't believe what I was seeing. It was very frightening. We learned later that some cars were hit on that road."

They went to his aunt and uncle's house on his father's side. They stayed for the 16 days of the war's duration. Though their fear would escalate when they heard Israeli fighter jets pass overhead, they were not in the line of fire. In Sidon, they awaited news of the war's end so they could return home. Walid recalls at that time hearing about a terrible incident in Qana, a village in southern Lebanon where there were United Nations tents to provide safe haven for those who had fled their homes. It was bombed by the Israeli ships, and several civilians were killed or wounded.

According to various news reports, the Israeli government later stated in a U.N. investigation that (1) it was firing on Hezbollah military positions that were identified to be nearby in response to them firing mortars at Israeli positions, and (2) it was unaware that a refugee camp was being used in Qana. This report contained various conflicting details, though the Israeli government did express regret and remorse for the resulting destruction of life. Nonetheless, the war enhanced the animosity of many in Lebanon toward Israel. It also raised questions about the Hezbollah's tactics of being among civilians during battle. For Walid and his family, it was a continuation of conflict and destruction that could arise at any moment in their country.

At the age of eight, he had experienced the first of many wars. In Tyr, he recalls seeing bombed-out buildings that had been intact before this. The bakery they had frequented was gone, as were other places that had been so familiar. There were warnings to stay away from cluster bombs unexploded on the ground. It continued to be a frightening time for Walid and his family. It began to be the norm in Lebanon.

Conflict in Lebanon could be seen almost every day. Even from his father's restaurant, he recalls, one could see the mountains to the south where there were Israeli checkpoints, and they could see Hezbollah attacks followed by Israeli helicopters retaliating.

The surreal nature of this existence was a reality, and the people of Lebanon accepted this as part of their day-to-day lives.

"When you are living that life, you just adapt. Sometimes we'd go to the beach and some military activity was taking place, so we'd just go home. It was almost routine. Strange to think about it that way, but that's how it was," Walid reflects.

The Israelis withdrew in 2000, when Walid was twelve.

Although he had become numb to that existence, his youngest sister could not avoid her anxiety. Any sound frightened her. She cried a lot.

"Before the youngest sister was born, the other sisters [had been] there with the Israeli invasion of Lebanon in 1982. They lived in Beirut with my parents at that time. They saw tanks crushing cars and often everyone had to evacuate to the beach. After that war ended, they did not experience the mental stress the way my youngest sister did."

When asked how he felt about the Israelis, he said that he hated them when he was younger. Everyone did, he says.

"As I grew up," he says, "I took a different perspective. I don't blame Israel. Palestinians from Lebanon shelling Israel on a daily basis justified Israel doing what it did to protect themselves. I don't blame them. But in the Middle East, propaganda breeds hate. I read a lot and thought a great deal about what took place in the region. This allowed me to step away from the typical information being fed to most Arabs in the Middle East to form my own conclusions. My hope is that future generations on all sides will be able to see clearly enough to bring about peace."

Walid says that Hezbollah is a big part of Lebanese life. Although they are Shia Muslim, most people from all religions in Lebanon support them. They are viewed as heroes. However, he recognizes that, before 2000, they were more respected. He says they lost their purpose by shifting their support to

Palestine instead of maintaining a neutrality that would be helpful to stabilizing Lebanon.

Walid says that many Lebanese believe that Palestine is a Palestinian problem. Yasser Arafat and his military wing occupied Lebanon in 1982, and no one was happy with the Palestinians, who were Sunni. They hated Shia, and this was reflected in their harsh treatment of Lebanese people.

In 2005, the former prime minister of Lebanon, Rafik Hariri, was assassinated in a massive car bombing that killed 21 others, as well. Hariri was respected by many in Lebanon and by many leaders worldwide. He was Sunni but seen as supportive of all sects and religions. Walid remembers that this was a very sad time for the citizens of Lebanon. Internal strife of this magnitude shook the country in ways not felt during conflict with Israel. This seemed to change the fabric of political and religious relations significantly.

Walid recalls that, because of the assassination, school was cancelled for a week. The country was in mourning. Tension between Sunni and Shia escalated like never before. The Sunni believed that Syria (which was supported by Hezbollah) was behind the car bomb that killed Hariri. He had been opposed to Syria's involvement and influence in Lebanon. Syrian president Bashar al Assad had reportedly threatened Hariri if he tried to undermine Syria's role in Lebanon, and it was not until a U.N.-backed tribunal in 2013 — following extensive investigation over eight years after the assassination — that some members of Hezbollah were indicted for the murder.

A new war with Israel in 2006 erupted after Hezbollah sent rockets into Israel as a diversion that led to abducting soldiers to be used in exchange for Lebanese soldiers imprisoned in Israel. The war lasted 34 days, ending with a U.N.-brokered cease fire.

At the outset of the war, Lebanese citizens found themselves, once again, in the position of bracing themselves for what was to come.

Walid recalls that his and other families now needed to stock up on supplies. He remembers that he went to the bakery to buy a lot of bread and to a store to get enough milk for his family and to purchase other goods. Once again, Lebanon was at war.

He recalls, "At one point I went out onto my grandparents' balcony and counted 37 Israeli fighter jets flying overhead."

During the beginning of that war, they mostly remained in the shelter. At night, in particular, they would emerge from the confines of their enclosure only to see bombs strafing the star-filled sky. Fear rippled throughout Tyr and all of Lebanon.

After their fifth day in the shelter, Walid's family made the decision to evacuate their city. A fuel station nearby filled with propane had been hit by a missile, causing a deafening explosion and fireball that lit up the night. They had no choice but to leave, they realized.

"We saw it. I remember it was a humid summer night, typical of many such nights in Tyr, and we had come out to get some air. About two miles away the explosion happened. We could see the fire and smoke. There was no way we would be able to sleep. We couldn't even go down to the shelter. We were in shock. All three sisters were there, even my sister who had come from Nigeria to visit with her infant. So was my sister from America who also was just visiting."

Their plan was to take three separate cars.

Walid explains, "We separated all of the family members into the cars. I drove the middle sister, her infant son, and my mom. We knew that we were taking a risk by leaving, but we felt that we had to. We also determined to do it this way so that if any of the cars was hit by a missile at least we would have some survivors."

There was no time to process the enormity of this decision. They just had to move as quickly away from Tyr as possible.

"It was an exhausting drive," he says. "We went to the mountains where the Druze lived to a city called Barook. We figured that there was nothing of importance there for the Israelis to want to attack. My father was friends with Walid Jumblatt, who is a world-renowned Druze political leader in Lebanon. It was he who arranged to have us stay in his city."

He remembers the fear he felt about rockets hitting them. He drove fast, knowing that he had to get there so as to be enveloped by the relative safety of the mountains.

"On my way I got a call from a friend who was also my colleague. I had been a firefighter then, and he called to tell me that the fire department had been bombed. He said everyone was dead. I was in disbelief. I couldn't imagine this horror. I felt helpless."

Walid didn't know what to do. He was crying and shaken. But he had to get his family to safety. When they arrived in Barook, one of his father's other friends, a judge, took them into his home.

They saw on TV news that Walid's fire department, on the first floor, was not affected in the devastating way described by his friend. Still, significant damage and destruction had occurred. The jet fighter's missile had hit the top of the fourteen-story building, and many were killed. Oddly, a truck parked next to the fire department literally kept that part of the structure from toppling. Tragically, however, one of his colleagues had a two-year-old daughter who was killed in the daycare on the top floor. The grief and anguish that he felt permeated his every pore.

His grandmother's sister, who lived in an apartment right behind the building, happened to be near a window when a shard of glass was propelled at her as a result of the explosion and was embedded into her stomach. Two days later she died in the hospital.

Walid's grandparents Abo Yousef and Alia remained in Tyr. The worried family was frantic to get them out. After trying to find someone to take them, they were finally able to pay a truck driver to drive them to Barook.

"We were all so nervous waiting for them to arrive and calling their cell phone every ten minutes because at that time many of the bridges were destroyed and roads were extremely dangerous. Luckily, they made it safely, and we were overjoyed to see them."

Walid felt a lot of guilt being in Barook and not Tyr. He was torn. He had "a lot on my plate," he says.

"In some ways I thought that I should have been with my fellow firefighters. I wanted to help out the people who remained in Tyr. I also felt an obligation to take care of my family while in Barook. It was a very difficult time for me emotionally."

On the thirteenth day of the war, there was an evacuation plan for U.S. citizens. Walid and his sisters were citizens, but his sister Tala's baby had not come with any documentation from Nigeria, so Tala could not leave. Walid's father decided to stay with Tala and the baby, so they remained in Barook when the rest left hastily. Walid, his two other sisters and their children, and his mother went by boat to Cyprus, where they were first sent to a refugee camp. Each camp had thousands of refugees. Fortunately, Walid and his family remained there for only a short time before taking a plane to Frankfurt, Germany, where they remained in the airport overnight. They then flew to Newark, New Jersey, and on to Salt Lake City. The dizzying journey culminated with them making their own reservations to fly from there to San Francisco where, just south of the city, his aunt and uncle lived.

Finally they were in familiar territory. It was here Walid had spent more than a few summers. After a short time in that house, they moved into his sister and husband's home nearby for two months, awaiting transit back to Lebanon.

"We were watching the news day and night, seeing all my friends at the fire department extinguishing fires and pulling people out of the rubble. I questioned myself a lot: why did I leave them and flee to safety, am I not as courageous as them?"

When Walid did return to Lebanon a few months later, it was a terrifying reunion. The whole country was decimated.

While still in high school, a senior, he joined a U.N. group as the chief medic to oversee ten units whose mission was to disable or destroy cluster bombs and other unexploded ordinance. Typically dropped by aircraft, cluster bombs are meant to explode just prior to reaching the ground, thus saturating an area the size of several football fields and killing or injuring anyone within range. Often, some of the bombs dropped land unexploded on the ground, but they are no less a threat: should they be disturbed, they can explode.

Each team had nine searchers, a medic, and an expert in bombs. Even at Walid's young age, he had several years of studying and working as a paramedic. Because of this, he was tapped to supervise the other medical personnel, including two doctors.

"In one of the villages, Bet Yahoun, we were one of the first units to enter to search for the cluster bombs. It was like driving into Chernobyl. It was abandoned, cold, burned-out buildings and cars. I have such a clear memory of this. As we searched the village, we found some [bombs] that could be disabled, and some that had to be detonated. We had to be focused on our jobs, because if we truly took in what we were involved in I don't think we could have done it," Walid recalls.

Another vivid memory surfaces as Walid thinks about this time in his life. He was near a city called Marja'youn when he got a call from the main office that two supervising medics had been injured by ground mines when they tried to help a local shepherd. Two colleagues were at the scene when Walid arrived. One was a friend, who ran to greet him with a huge hug. It was as if salvation had arrived. His friend was shaking as he had not been tasked with tending to such an acute and horrific medical emergency to that point. Walid's medic training kicked into gear, and he was able to stabilize the men, who were bleeding profusely. Still, the two injured supervisors went to a nearby hospital, where both required amputation of their legs below the knee.

The story of what had befallen the two men clearly depicts the compassion that Walid and the teams showed throughout the six months they were tasked to do this work.

After serving in this unit, Walid returned to Tyr to finish high school. However, normalcy — a sense of stability and routine — was not to return with him. He finished high school because an administrator that his family knew made sure of it. However, Walid was unable to concentrate. He felt depressed, anxious, and detached from the world around him. He acknowledges that, looking back, he believes he was experiencing

Post Traumatic Stress Syndrome, but this was not diagnosed or treated.

"I didn't feel normal. I couldn't concentrate, and felt obligated to do my homework, but that was about it. I felt separate from my high school experiences. School was not important. I had developed a totally different perspective on life. Seeing all that I had seen made me depressed; at times almost hopeless."

He went to college right after high school and studied Business Administration Management at the Lebanese American University of Beirut. His father had wanted him to go to the United States for college, but he didn't want to leave his family. By that time, he was feeling more connected to his studies and to people around him. He buried his prior experiences in order to move on, he acknowledges.

While in college, especially in 2010, there were clashes between Shia, Sunni, Druze, and Christians. The segregation was real. They would sit in separate sections of the classrooms, dining halls, and generally all over campus. There was a lot of tension. Walid was even involved in physical fights between groups as a member of the Shia sect. He acknowledges that he felt a great deal of pent-up anger.

When he was a sophomore in college, the head of police intelligence, who was Sunni, was assassinated, creating even deeper divides. The Sunni blamed the Shia and Syria. Police came to quell riots at the university. Rocks, bottles, and other projectiles were thrown. The intensity of emotions on all sides boiled over.

Hezbollah supported the Shia and participated in "protecting" their students by having cars of armed militants nearby the university campus.

Walid recalls a time that he was driving home from class and traffic had stopped on the highway. Extremist Sunnis were burning tires and throwing them toward cars, and pointing guns at drivers. He was jolted into a heightened state of fear.

"One man approached my car and I had my gun ready to defend myself. I saved himself by showing them that my name was Walid, which is a typical Sunni name. He let me go, but I had to turn my car around and drive against the stopped traffic to escape. It took four hours to drive through mountain passes to get back to Beirut. I could not go to Tyr because there was no access."

When he graduated in 2012, he and his girlfriend at the time decided they wanted to get married, but he needed a job first. In Lebanon there was no work even with his bachelor's degree in Business Administration Management.

With no other viable option, he went to the United States to work with his brother-in-law in his car dealership, but they didn't get along. After two and half months, he returned Tyr. Besides, he missed his family and his girlfriend.

In 2013, a friend of his had told him of work in Iraq, so Walid went to Bagdad. His father knew someone who was a retired general from Korea. He had an oil company, and Walid became his agent in representing the company's concern in the region. Traveling back and forth between Lebanon and Iraq for the company became burdensome, and it was not a fruitful venture for Walid, so he resigned.

Walid muses, "I feel incredibly lucky that this didn't work out. ISIS arrived soon after I left. Who knows what would have happened?"

The year 2013 was a depressing time for Walid. He couldn't find stable work in Tyr, and it was also a time of unrest in Beirut. Suicide bombings were taking hold of that city, and any semblance of normalcy was gone. In addition, Syrian refugees had flooded the country because of the humanitarian crisis confronting them in their home country. Walid felt defeated.

In 2014, gathering his resilience as best as he could, he went to Nigeria to work. According to his sister and her husband, and after doing his own research, there was a need for poultry farms in the country. However, he eventually came to the realization that it required a huge financial investment, which he did not have nor could he access what was needed, and the risk of trying to move further on this venture was too high. After five months, he returned to Lebanon and subsequently broke up with his girlfriend. Despondent as he now felt, one more opportunity was on the horizon.

In February 2015, he was contacted by a cousin in Northern California who asked him to join his high-end used-car business. His sister invited him to stay with her and her daughter, so he could be near the business. He accepted the offer, moved to California, and has not looked back since.

He has also not been back to Lebanon. He has a girlfriend here now and is in the happiest time of his life for as long as he can remember.

He has struggled with anxiety and depression in America, to be sure. How could he not, with all that he has seen and lived through in his life? He says he had negative thoughts about how disastrous the world is. Yet, since moving to America, he has felt a greater sense of calm and safety, and he is more sure of himself. He feels more respected.

"I am honest and I work hard. That's the thing about America. It allows those of us who want to, to succeed. In other countries, corruption is the norm. Paying off police and politicians, and greed is as routine as brushing your teeth."

He misses his parents, sister, and grandmother. His father is not healthy enough to travel, and his mother is the caregiver for her mother, who has Alzheimer's disease.

Walid opines, "I don't want to return to Lebanon. The memories are too sharp and painful, and there really is nothing for me there. I have made a life here, and it is here that I am at peace."

In Germany during World War II, most citizens did not protest Hitler's plans to invade Europe. This included his plans to annihilate Jews, whom he blamed for all of Germany's economic woes. Still, there were pockets of resistance, and a sense by many as the war progressed that they were increasingly at the mercy of the horrors of war. Toward the end of the war, it became evident that Germans were feeling the brunt of food-rationing, a collapsing economy, and the specter of widespread poverty. Its citizens had now become targets of the Allies' regular bombing, and, at war's end, especially in Eastern Europe where many ethnic Germans had fled (as they believed it to be safer from the Allied attacks), advancing Russian troops committed atrocities against them that mirrored the Nazis' brutality against Jews and others they deemed inferior. Survival became the modus operandi for many Germans.

Heidi

Heidi was from a small town in Germany called Beztdorf. She was born during World War II in 1944 into a family whose ancestry was deeply rooted in the regions that her parents came from. On her maternal grandmother's side, her relatives had lived for generations on the French border near Alsace and the Rhine River, and to this day they remain vintners. Heidi's father's family came from the Black Forest, and they spanned generations of dairy farmers.

When her mother was a teenager, in the early years of World War II, she had lived in the city of Cologne and worked in her uncle's hotel. But, as the war intensified and Cologne became a target of Allied bombing, it was too dangerous a place for her to live. She moved back to Betzdorf to live with her mother, grandmother, and aunt. There she spotted a soldier she had seen earlier, when she was just 15, and had been smitten by. He soon became her boyfriend, her lover, and eventually her husband.

Heidi's parents were married in 1944, but her mother, Anna, had already given birth to their daughter some months before that. Her father, Rainer, was away, fighting for Germany on the Russian front, so Anna and Heidi stayed in the little town where the family had lived for so many generations. Anna and Rainer didn't see each other until he got "leave" and would come to visit. The practice of being pregnant before marriage was not so unusual during war time. Because of the uncertainty and anxiety about the safety and subsequent return from the war for many soldiers and their girlfriends, it was often the case that couples consummated their relationships, resulting in the births of these "war babies." When Anna's parents realized that she was pregnant, they decided to have a proxy wedding. Rainer had his commanding officer validate the marriage while he was on the Russian front, and Anna received a marriage document from the *bürgermeister* (mayor). Later, when Rainer returned from the war zone on leave, they had civil and religious ceremonies. He again left and then returned for a visit when Heidi was three months old.

Prior to and after giving birth, Anna was deemed by the German authorities to be one of the many able-bodied women who were conscripted to dig trenches at the French border in support of the German soldiers. She was twenty years old at the time, pregnant, and her baby's father was fighting in Russia. Heidi recalls her mother reflecting on how outspoken she was and how she resisted German authority. Her verbal protestations and her absence some days from the trench-digging job resulted in threats that she would be made to "disappear."

Anna wrote numerous letters and post cards to her husband that included questions and commentaries she knew were being censored by the Nazis, according to Heidi's recollection of her mother's wartime stories. This correspondence brought German authorities to her door, and they would pepper her with questions; more than once they threatened to have her "punished" for speaking out against the Fatherland.

Anna also told Heidi that, when Allied bombers dropped their payload nearby, she would grab her daughter and they would race for cover in the hills. In the vineyards were bunkers where the town's population would seek shelter underground. In her mother's recounting of the war, one prominent theme arises for Heidi: above all, one had to survive.

After her father returned to the Russian front when Heidi was three months old, news arrived that he was missing. Heidi was only a year old at the time. Her grandmother later recalled for Heidi that her mother was inconsolable. For many years, Anna held onto the hope that his death was not true, that he would come knocking on the door at any moment. Eventually, his superior officer sent Anna a letter stating that the last time Leopold had been seen was in battle. So, in 1945 he was declared missing in action, and after seven years he was officially considered dead.

For Heidi and her family immediately after the war, food was scarce, and threats to their survival were confronted on a daily basis. Because they were living under French occupation, the Moroccan army was sent to oversee their town. Sexual assault was rampant. Heidi's mother would tell stories about how all the women in town had to hide so as to avoid attacks. After a number of months, the soldiers left, likely due to the protestations of the townspeople to the French of their treatment by the Moroccans.

Heidi recalls that she and her grandmother would stand in long lines to get a loaf of bread at the bakery. She speaks of shivering in the cold and of the pangs of hunger. They would use rationing cards given by the newly installed government. She was considered an orphan, and had a card to show this, because her father didn't return from the war. This gave her family a little extra bread.

Betzdorf consisted predominantly of farms, so people from the surrounding cities would come to barter their silverware and jewelry in exchange for farm products. Bartering for food became a way of life for many.

In 1948, Anna went back to Cologne to work in her grandfather's hotel. She returned on some weekends to visit. Heidi, at the age of five, occasionally took the train on her own and met her mother in Cologne to stay for a time.

"Today it would be completely unacceptable, if not illegal, to send a child at such a young age by train alone. My mother would arrange for the conductor to make sure that I made it safely to the Cologne train station where she would meet me. My joy at being with her was unmistakable," Heidi remembers.

It was during one of Anna's brief visits to Betzdorf that she met Georg, a fellow townsman she knew from childhood, who she began dating, and a man who would eventually become Heidi's stepfather.

Georg's father immigrated to the United States years before his son would arrive. Although they had been estranged from each other, Georg agreed to join him in 1951 viewing this as a needed change from war-torn Germany and a place to find safety and opportunity. He agreed to move in with his father if Anna and Heidi could eventually join him, too.

In 1951, Georg moved to Middletown, New York. In 1953, when Heidi was age 9, she and her mother arrived there, too. It was a bittersweet move because she had left her grandmother, with whom she was very close, back in Germany. It broke both their hearts. Eventually, her grandmother and aunt did immigrate to New Rochelle, New York, where Anna, Georg, and Heidi would later live. A family of strong women had survived and had made it to America.

Heidi recalls, "One of the biggest events for me was coming over on the S.S. America in second class. The array of food was mind boggling. Even though the area I grew up in was a region that had orchards and other bounty, the tropical fruit was almost magical."

She also vividly remembers what it was like to go to her first supermarket. The choices and options were overwhelming to her. It was so unlike what she had experienced all of her early life in Germany.

However, the relief of being away from Germany soon dissipated. Georg's father is described by Heidi as "almost abusive." She recalls that he used his son and wife like indentured servants. For example, "Georg's father took in boarders to bring in extra income. It was a huge Victorian house with several rooms. He threatened that if my mother did not clean, cook, and do the laundry, and basically provide for these boarders, she and her family would be sent back to Germany. In addition to the servitude, they had to pay rent."

Georg was a mechanic during the day and drove his father's taxi at night. When Anna would protest about how unfair this was, Georg's father would lord over them the threats of deportation if she didn't like it.

Fortunately, her parents joined a night-school class to learn English, and there they met a number of other German emigres. About a year into their class, an immigration lawyer came to speak with the class. They asked him if Georg's father could actually have them deported, to which the lawyer affirmatively stated that he could not since they were legal residents.

Their fears allayed, Georg and Anna decided that it was time to leave Middletown. It was also at this time that Heidi's half-brother Thomas, who is eleven years younger, was born.

Her parents were very hard working. Georg was good at fixing things. He had an innate talent for repairing complicated mechanical issues despite the fact that he left school after the eighth grade.

Heidi had a conflicted relationship with Georg for a long time, especially during her teen years. She describes him as a very gentle and loving man. Still, the idealized image of her own father loomed large.

Growing up in Germany with beautiful photos in their apartment of this dashing, blond haired, blue-eyed figure, and being told that he was an amazing man who brought joy to everyone he encountered, made it impossible for Heidi to accept Georg as her father. She says that she was not disrespectful but that she had a more distant relationship with him.

"I never called him my father. In fact, I never called him anything. It was not until I became an adult that I realized what a sweet man he really was."

When they left Middletown and moved to Scarsdale downstate, Heidi was in seventh grade. Her assimilation into the American way of life would now be tested as she was confronted by her German heritage.

Her school experience in Middletown had been very positive. English came to her quickly. Her family had been surrounded by other German immigrants who provided an affiliation, comfort, and connection.

Their move to Scarsdale was encouraged by a close German friend who told her parents that there was a position available on a beautiful estate where they could live for free in exchange for Georg maintaining the property. They moved into a tiny cottage on the grounds of the estate. Her parents slept on the couch in the living room, and Heidi and her brother each had a small bedroom. Soon thereafter, her grandmother moved to the United States, so the elderly woman and Thomas shared his bedroom.

Georg converted an unused part of the cottage into a bedroom for Heidi. Her parents continued to sleep in the living room.

Heidi says, "It was a beautiful environment. The owners of the estate would leave the country for three or four months every year, so it felt like it was ours. We had parties and celebrated many events there."

Still, she was seen as "the gardener's daughter" by those who lived nearby. There were many wealthy Jewish families in and around Scarsdale, and Heidi was now confronted with two facts: her family was not well-off, and (more significantly) she was a native German.

Her brother, who was born in America, was nevertheless tormented by some older boys for being German. He was sometimes called a Nazi, and once a swastika was painted on the driveway. This caused the family, but especially Thomas, many anxiety-filled moments.

Heidi laments, "Poor Thomas — he didn't have a clue. He had never even been to Germany. His confusion and angst were very sad to us all."

It was during this period that Heidi began to explore newsreels and books about the Holocaust. She would ask her parents and grandmother about it, as well. Heidi wanted to know what the Nazis actually did. Her hunger to learn about this was voracious.

The answers from her parents and grandmother were that they didn't know about the atrocities while they were going on. They just knew that the Jews who had come to their town to buy goods stopped coming.

Heidi describes how she felt ashamed of being German and that she no longer wanted to be German. Her identity was in turmoil.

"Our family was part of a group of Germans living in New Rochelle. We had parties, celebrated occasions together, and stayed close to them," she says. However, Heidi began to distance herself emotionally from them.

She had a best friend, Inge, whom she had met when she was 13, who herself had been in a family that had a similar experience. Inge did discuss fleeing the Russians and going to refugee camps, but no one discussed the Holocaust. Heidi also never had this discussion with her American friends. In those days little was mentioned about the Holocaust in any circles.

She wasn't taunted or bullied like her brother. However, she still had post-war memories of when she was in Germany. She had lived it, and she had also heard her family's stories of deprivation, loss, and fear. She wasn't angry at her family and didn't even ask them to justify why they did nothing to stop the Holocaust, knowing that this was not a realistic question.

In fact, in response to Heidi's angst over what had transpired in Germany, her mother told her "You learn to keep your mouth shut. If you don't want to be accused of being a traitor where you could be sent away or worse, you kept quiet."

Heidi came to the realization that basic survival took hold for many Germans during the war. It's not that those Germans had no role in the genocide that Hitler unleashed, it's just that as the war progressed they were all confronted with deprivation.

Nevertheless, seeing the pictures of Auschwitz and the other atrocities horrified her. Trying to understand how this could happen in her country, or any country for that matter, was too difficult to comprehend. Her empathy for those destroyed by the Holocaust grew in enormity.

One of the other things she learned that stunned her was that her great-uncle, whom she had never met, was the attorney who had been chosen to defend Adolf Eichmann, the Nazi high official who orchestrated "the final solution" to eradicate the Jews and was being prosecuted in Israel, later to be hanged. He had previously defended Nazis at the Nuremburg Trials.

"I became very sensitive, aware, and embracing of Judaism. When I have the opportunity to go to a synagogue, I go. Most of my friends today are Jewish. The first bar mitzvah I went to was overwhelming, more so than any experience I had in a church or cathedral. On top of that, I [later] married a Jewish man."

After ten years in New Rochelle, she moved out and went to college. She got married to a man who was Catholic (and "crazy," says Heidi) but divorced eight years later. They had two children. Five years after the divorce, she married Jess, who is Jewish, and they have been together for 35 years.

The journey Heidi took — her awakening and exploration of German guilt and processing the mark it has left on her, and the subsequent "awakening" as she terms it — were fostered as she grew up in America after leaving the ruins of her home country. She is at peace now, at least to the extent she can be, having reconciled personal guilt and shame but recognizing the horrors of where she came from, for which she bears no responsibility but to which she will forever be connected.

Following World War II, the Yalta Conference, which was attended by British Prime Minister Winston Churchill, Soviet Premier Joseph Stalin, and U.S. President Franklin D. Roosevelt, resulted in a new order in Europe. The conference produced an agreement that Germany would be divided into three zones of occupation run by those three countries and France. Stalin promised free elections in Eastern Europe, as well. But that never happened, and Soviet domination in that region remained until countries began to slowly and sometimes violently exit. Czechoslovakia was no exception.

Eva

Eva was born in 1951 in Prague, Czechoslovakia, a country in which her family had lived for many generations. Her grandparents lived in a town called Budweiser, where they established a business they called Petrof Piano. Eva explains that, though those pianos were not as famous as Steinways, they were still recognized as beautifully constructed instruments that were more affordable. Her grandmother had a sister who was a world-renowned pianist. However, business went dormant during the Nazi occupation in World War II.

Living under the rule of Hitler's Germany made it hard on the citizens of her country; there was widespread poverty. Later, Eva's grandmother told her that she had witnessed Jews being shipped to concentration camps, and that the sadness and fear felt by her and others was pervasive. Things were so dismal that the grandmother even had her nose measured by the occupying Nazis, which was one of the practices of the time, to see if she was Jewish.

Eva says, "Czech people never fight. They have survived many political aggressions and oppression in their history. Inside they may not agree, but they bend to power. There may be resistance, but it is often secretive and hidden."

For a few years after the war, Czechoslovakia was the most democratic country in Eastern Europe. But then the Yalta Conference resulted in giving control of Czechoslovakia to the Soviet Union. Under communism, houses of worship were closed, since religion was seen as an evil. Although Eva's family members were not particularly religious Protestants, their occasional observance was stopped when Stalin imposed his dictates on Eastern Europe.

Following the war, Jews in Eastern Europe began to drift toward communism. Worn out by the Holocaust, and feeling supported by the Soviet's victory over Germany on their border, Jews hoped that this was a system that would be open to their way of life. However, the non-Jewish communists attacked the Jews, promoting all of the stereotypes and envy that predicate antisemitism. An ugly brand of communist rule emerged.

Eva's grandparents on her mother's side were arrested and jailed for being anti-communist. Her grandmother was imprisoned for three years and her grandfather for two years beginning in 1950. The government confiscated their property and their business. Their crime: having a son who actively resisted communist takeover. Their son, Eva's uncle, risked his life by helping Czech citizens defect. He would sneak people across the border to Germany in order to escape communist rule. However, he was eventually arrested and imprisoned for 13 years; he was put in a labor camp and forced to work under incredibly harsh conditions.

Eva did not know him until he was released. She was 16 when she met him, and she recalls that he was gaunt, had no teeth, and looked depleted of life.

Eva was young when her mother took her to visit her grandmother in jail. She recalls that her grandmother gave her a little yarn doll that she had made in prison, and she also vividly remembers her grandmother waving goodbye out of the jailhouse window. Yet what she mostly remembers is the fear she felt in the gray, cold, dank prison and the sadness that it lodged deep in her soul.

Eva credits her grandmother for giving her the strength to carry through many tough times. Despite all of the hardships her grandmother endured, and despite their freedom being diminished, she was the one making lemonade out of lemons. It was she who instilled a feeling of hope against all odds, to never give up.

Following the release of Eva's grandfather from jail, he was allowed to build pianos again because there were few master craftsmen like him. Of course, the results of his craftsmanship were then given to a government office that sold the instruments to profit the Communist Party.

Even given all that her family suffered, Eva says she had a happy life. There was singing, laughing, and reading in her home. It was a refuge of sorts. She would also go to her other grandmother's house in the country to eat rabbit and fresh vegetables, and to enjoy being away from the harshness of Prague.

Outside of her home, the city was very different. Confronted by the ills of communism, she often felt great angst. In school, her teachers would take her aside and warn her not to utter anti-government sentiments as her reputation for being outspoken about her opinions of communism was being noticed.

She recalls that one day in school as a 10-year-old, she pronounced that America must be doing pretty well because on their dollar bill it says "In God We Trust." Her teacher asked where she heard this, and she replied that her father had admired America and showed her a picture of the dollar.

The teacher responded that America was not doing well because the phrase on the dollar proved that they were oppressed by religion and didn't understand the higher elements of science because of this belief. Eva disagreed and would not back down. This contributed to the mounting evidence that Eva was not "a good communist."

She recalls, "They tried to brainwash us about the greatness of the Soviet Union and communism. When I was younger I even believed some of their propaganda. One day I came home and told my father that we should move to the Soviet Union. He nearly slapped me. It seems we lived a double life. My father told me about truth and freedom. He secretly learned much through Radio-free Europe. The volume had to be low so that no one would hear and report him. He told me not to tell anyone about this. Sometimes I couldn't help myself though, and in a fit of defiance would denounce our country's way of life. That didn't always endear me to those who did believe in the communist doctrine. I eventually learned not to say too much, so that I wouldn't get my parents in trouble."

Her father was a trained mechanical engineer. However, the government did not allow him to practice his trade. Instead, he was made to repair refrigerators, and he would come home feeling the effects of the Freon gas. He almost seemed high on drugs, she recalls. It was surely not a healthy environment for him. Her mother was a piano teacher, but she was made to sell shoes per the government's requirements. Eva's grandmother had to work in a motorcycle manufacturing plant with dangerous, sharp metal parts. None of their work was by choice; all of it was forced upon them by "the party."

Because Eva was the oldest child, with a younger sister and brother, her father seemed to favor her in some ways. He taught her English and gave her American literature. She always had the notion that he wanted to move to America, but she wasn't aware of the plans that her parents were developing, which would be revealed much later. If their plans leaked in any way, they could have been jailed.

In 1967, with the Communist Party weakening, some travel restrictions were loosened. Eva's mother and brother applied to go visit a relative in Switzerland, and their request was approved by the government.

At the same time, Eva was told by her mother of a family friend who lived in London whom Eva was to visit. He was seen as a hero in that he was Czech but had been a resistance fighter against the Nazis in England. Eva applied for a travel visa and then went to visit him in London. She didn't know until she got there, from a letter her mother sent, that her father and sister went to Yugoslavia. Because Yugoslavia was in the Soviet sphere, the Czech government didn't suspect that the family was planning a defection. But her father and his younger daughter snuck across the border into Austria, and into freedom. Her mother implored Eva not to return to Prague, that a plan was afoot to go to America.

However, unbeknownst to her parents, the family friend, whom Eva refers to as her uncle, was a sexual predator.

Eva says, "He made life very frightening for me. He lied. He said he lived with a wife, but he had no wife. I was 16, he was 45, and he tried to touch me and sexually assault me. My parents didn't know what he was like. I had a knife under my pillow, so that if he further tried to harm me I would kill him. I would go out into London for as long as I could to not be near him. Returning to his home was always a horrible feeling. He eventually left me alone, realizing that I was not going to succumb to his attempts at sexual assault."

Eva reminds me that, at this time, the police would not have done anything had she tried to press charges. She had to fend for herself.

Despite her mother's written pleas not to leave London and go back to Prague, since they were going to meet up in Switzerland and go to America, Eva needed to go back to her homeland, even if it meant communist Czechoslovakia.

She recalls, "My mother sent me a few letters instructing me not to leave. I didn't open the letters because I knew what she wanted to tell me. After two months of enduring my uncle's harassment, I got him to take me to the airport so I could go back to Prague. I didn't want to return to communist Czechoslovakia, but this man made me so miserable that I couldn't stay there any longer."

Eva reveals at this point that her relationship with her mother was not always very good. Her mother could be accusatory, perfectionistic, and cold. When Eva wrote from Prague to tell her mother all that had transpired in London and why she needed to leave, her mother accused her of lying. Eva describes how angry and rejected she felt.

"My mother turned away from me. She didn't believe me. I was a pretty girl, and age 16, [so] she assumed that I did something to provoke him. Her disbelief of me changed my life forever. My father, who I had been very close with, seemed to not want to go against what my mother was saying. This rejection was very hard on me."

Back in Prague, teachers praised her. "Eva returned," they said. They thought that she came to realize that communism was the right way of life.

It would be another thirteen years before she'd see her parents and siblings again. She had one tearful phone call with her parents when they were in Vienna, before they left for America. But even her father did not speak to her by phone, or write to her, for ten years. She had no word from him at all during that time,

Fortunately, her grandparents were still in Czechoslovakia, and they helped her out as best they could. Just knowing that her loving grandparents were there gave her solace. She was soon able to get her parents' apartment back.

Yet Eva was under the watchful eye of the police. She was interrogated every couple of months about why her parents defected. She could be picked up any time the police decided that they needed to speak with her.

In 1968, the new leader of Czechoslovakia, Alexander Dubcek, attempted some reforms of the Communist Party. As he himself coined it, "socialism with a human face" was to be the new norm. He lifted censorship of the media and opened up society so that people felt freer than they had in many years. Eva was so hopeful that she even wrote to her parents to say that they should return. Her mother wrote to encourage her to immigrate to New York where they now lived, saying that the change in Czechoslovakia would only be temporary. Eva replied that the feeling of freedom was real and palpable, and that her family should be part of this new era.

This optimism turned out to be short-lived.

"I was giddy with freedom and possibilities," she says, "but my denial of the reality that the Soviet Union would ever allow this to take hold came back to haunt me."

In 1969, Soviet tanks rolled into Prague, and harsh rule reappeared. The fervent hope that Eva and many others felt was dissolved in an instant. The new military dictator was charged with enforcing a return to strict communist rule. Tanks were swarming the city, and the darkness that had so punctuated the past had reemerged.

The authorities knew a lot about Eva. Once, while being interrogated, she asked how they knew so much about her life. She was shown a large file of her perceived anti-communist activities.

She would make her requests to leave the country known on her required annual check-in visit to the authorities, or when she was picked up randomly for interrogation. Of course they refused to let her go. She would retort that, if she was an enemy of the state, wouldn't they want her out of the country? But this argument was met with scorn.

She wanted to go to college, but, because of her political background, she was not allowed to. Still, it was a requirement to work "for the good of society."

She found a job as a secretary with Czech Airlines. She had never typed a word in her life, but she learned on the job. It was a dull, lifeless existence, but at least it was a job.

Eva laughs as she describes one way she conquered the boredom.

"I would leave the office some days and ride the elevator up and down just to break the monotony of the job. I don't know how I lasted five years at that place."

She became very bitter about the state of affairs in Prague, and she lamented not leaving for America when she could have during the small window of opportunity in 1968.

In 1975, her maternal grandfather died, and her grandmother, who was now 70, left for America. Her paternal grandmother was still alive and living in the countryside with her flourishing garden. Otherwise, Eva had no other family nearby.

Also during this time, the secret police were more active than ever. Survival was the goal for most people living in Prague. Eva and her friends would go to pubs but couldn't say anything remotely anti-communist. They would go skiing or hiking to get away from the city, where they could talk freely and sing anti-communist songs.

Then, finally, she got some very good news: She learned that she would be allowed to attend junior college. So she left her job at the airline and began a program in art. The program director had to take a chance on her, knowing that her political beliefs were not in favor. He even said to her that he didn't know if he could accept her unless she did not speak about politics. She agreed to keep silent.

She loved studying art. She had newfound passion. To this day, she credits her art career to that school. She worked very hard in school, and indeed she was envied by some students because she was so prolific. Art was a way of expressing herself, and she did so with a vengeance. She could finally think clearly again after having been mentally tortured at her previous job.

When she communicated with her mother to tell her about art school, her mother denigrated her for doing "such an impractical thing." This only reinforced the sour relationship her mother perpetuated. Still, Eva refused to let this bring her down, and her resilience and strong sense of self would always lead her to a brighter place.

Finishing school allowed her to teach art. She got a part-time job and had enough money to pay the rent and buy food. It was a good job, but the government told her that she needed to have a full-time job — that she was taking food and doing other things that were denying others of their daily needs. Eva states that this was more of "their stupid rules that only denied people a truly happy life."

She was able to find a job as a cleaning woman in a supermarket. She would go in at 4:00 a.m., and her boss would stamp a government "work book" to document that she was working full time. She would be there just three or four hours, but it was viewed as "full time" as she was very efficient and fast at cleaning. She could then teach in the afternoons.

Eva says, "The work book acted as an identification card because the police could stop anyone on the streets anytime to check. If you didn't carry it and have the proper stamps, you could be arrested and interrogated."

One day, she was stopped by a police officer who asked how she came to be a cleaning lady when cleaning ladies were known to be prostitutes. She had to sign an affidavit stating that she was not a prostitute, but she had to endure the officer's ridicule for several hours at the police station.

In 1976, her sister sent her a book from America about macramé, and she showed it to her art students. Someone in her class informed on her to the authorities, and she was called in for interrogation. She had gotten the book from the United States, and this was seen as a subversive publication. She was told to stop teaching because she couldn't be trusted. This left her with only the cleaning job. The harshness that was the communist system continued to dominate her life.

This was the last straw for her; she had to leave Czechoslovakia. Eva, her boyfriend, and two other friends found out about someone who could provide them with false papers (for a price) to get out of the country and get them to Poland. From there, she believed, they could get permission to go to Sweden.

Eva says, "You didn't know who created the false papers. We never saw the person. Even though we got them, you never knew whether that person was going to actually turn you in."

The fear of what they were doing began to set in. But the harrowing journey to freedom was worth the risk, they believed.

Eva says, "Passengers on the train would ask what we were doing in Poland in the winter. We'd say that we were going to Sweden for a visit. We got to the Northern Sea and met up with a Swedish captain who was to take us. We almost succeeded."

A Polish policeman checked the papers and knew that they were false. He called the authorities in Prague to verify his discovery. Their plan had failed. They were then imprisoned in Poland for a difficult three months.

Eva recalls, "We were all separated and could not see each other. None of us spoke Polish, so communication was quite limited to say the least. They would interrogate me, but I didn't know what they were saying. I was in a cell with Polish prostitutes, not knowing when we'd get released. My safety was always at risk in the jail from assaults by the other prisoners. I had one prisoner who protected me though. She didn't want me to tell the guards that I was being threatened because she knew they would take it out on all of them with beatings."

She remembers thinking to herself, "You can jail me, but you cannot take away my thoughts!" It was this line of thinking that kept her strong.

When Eva and her friends were released, they were put on a train and sent to Warsaw. They were shackled, and the police had machine guns to keep them in line.

Eva smiles when she says: "The Polish Police were not very bright. They gave us our false papers back. Silently, my girlfriend and I were thinking the same thing. We were allowed to go to the bathroom, and inside we shredded the papers we had been given, but the boys we were with did not. I guess they were not so smart."

When they got to Prague, the police asked for their papers, but Eva and her girlfriend said that they never had false papers, so there was no proof of their crime against the Communist Party. After two weeks of harsh interrogation, they were released.

The authorities told Eva that she could no longer be jailed. They had no proof of anything. The friend she had traveled with had a father with some influence in the party. She believes that he made some calls about his daughter and Eva to get them released. The boys were released a few weeks later.

She got her old cleaning job back, but she wanted to leave the country more than ever.

In 1978, she went to the authorities again to see about going to America. The official said that she should go, that she was an enemy of the country. She was told to give up her citizenship, give up her property, pay for the remaining debt for art school, leave and never return.

"I couldn't believe what I was hearing," she says. "Was this a trick? Could I really finally go?"

She saw hundreds of people in the passport office who were labeled as dissidents and who were also "not able to be corrected."

It was a bureaucratic nightmare.

Her mother finally did something good for her, as she recalls. Her mother contacted Senator Jacob Javits of New York, who was able to work with the U.S. Embassy to get Eva the paperwork she needed to leave.

She had a boyfriend at the time who had left for Germany earlier.

Eva's nightmare didn't end, though.

"An angry German border officer pulled me off the train to check on my paperwork. My innate fear of anyone acting authoritarian quickly surfaced. He returned the paperwork after an hour, and reluctantly let me go."

She met her boyfriend in Munich, and they both left for America. He would eventually become her husband, and they had two children, though they divorced 17 years later.

While on the airplane, a passenger next to her asked why she was going to the United States. She told him why she was moving, and she could tell that he was touched.

When she arrived at her parents' house on Long Island, a large bouquet of flowers was on the doorstep, welcoming her to America; it had been sent to her by the kind stranger on the plane.

Eva was given a green card at the airport in New York, and she got her U.S. citizenship five years later.

She moved to upstate New York, to a small town in the Catskill Mountains, where she's been for over 30 years as an artist.

She loves where she lives now, and she feels comfortable and content with her life in this small, cozy town.

As she says, "In the Czech Republic today they live at the bottom of the bucket, and I am so happy that I got out. After what the country went through, I don't understand how they could now be reverting back to the right-wing politics of when I lived there. Remember, Czechs are people that bend to whatever authority is in power. It worries me that Europe is starting to head in the wrong direction. I also worry that I am seeing some of these trends here in America."

She writes an op-ed for a Czech magazine on a weekly basis to share her political views as someone having experienced a dreadful period of governmental repression.

For Eva today, at age 67, there is a feeling of gratitude for being welcomed here to live her life as she wishes. "That," she says, "is what truly makes America the great country it is, and should always strive to be."

The Union of Soviet Socialist Republics formed after the centuries-old Tsarist Russian Empire collapsed under the 1917 Russian Revolution. The U.S.S.R. became four socialist republics. In subsequent years, more republics were formed, and the country was the largest in the world, extending 8,650,000 square miles. It had a highly centralized government, meaning that "all roads" led to Moscow — and the Kremlin, where all political decisions were made to affect the entire union. However, after 1991, following democratic reforms by the government and the fall of the Berlin Wall, the independence movement of the Soviet states gained momentum. The Soviet government was unable to rein in the rapid changes taking place, and the Soviet Union dissolved.

Marina

Having grown up during the 1970s and 1980s in a small town on the Volga River about 65 miles outside of Moscow, Marina looks back longingly at her childhood home.

"It was beautiful," she says, "with lots of trees and greenery. Many wealthy people had summer homes along the river. It was a peaceful and almost idyllic place to live."

Her mother grew up in poverty in the Ural Mountains. Her father grew up in the mountains, as well, but from the North. He was a soldier and was stationed in her town — the town they still live in.

Marina's parents did not finish middle school because they had to work to support a family. Her three sisters were quite a bit older and lived away from home, so she was often on her own while her parents worked.

Married in 1959, her parents lived in the Soviet Union under Nikita Khrushchev and then Leonid Brezhnev; they only knew the ways of the communist system. The government provided for everyone. People worked the same job with little chance for promotion, but they got paid and were given apartments, food, and an expectation that theirs would be a modest, predictable life.

The messages they heard day-in and day-out were how wonderful the Soviet Union was, how grateful its citizens should be for what they had, and how evil the West was. This dogma had begun under the ruthless dictator Joseph Stalin. During his rule, from 1929 to 1953, the country endured World War II, but then, even after the war, millions more were killed throughout the country by Stalin's military and secret police, the KGB. It was also a time of one of the worst famines in human history.

Marina says, "Under Stalin, my mom's grandparents were greatly affected. They had a farm and were wealthy. They were killed by the military and all of their property was stolen."

Her grandmother would perpetuate a story that her own parents got sick and they died. The full extent of the awful truth was never revealed. Her mom didn't know much about it, either, only that they were killed.

Under Khrushchev, from 1958 to 1964, Soviet citizens were freed from the extreme authoritarian rule of Stalinism. Krushchev changed some of the government's repressive policies, and he sought a more peaceful relationship with the West. However, it was he who initiated the Cuban Missile Crisis in 1962 by placing nuclear weapons 90 miles from Florida. This set up a tense standoff with President John F. Kennedy, which almost led to a nuclear war, but it resulted in the USSR standing down and removing the missiles. It was also Khrushchev who had the Berlin Wall built to isolate communist East Germany, a part of the Soviet sphere, from democratic West Germany.

Marina's parents lived dutifully through all that the various phases of communism brought and through each new premiere or president. It was expected that their children would do the same.

The history of the Soviet Union for school children was noteworthy in its use of propaganda. It reflected the mindset that they lived the perfect life. Yet Marina recalls her life was far from perfect.

"Our history teachers promoted the myth through the books we had. I began to develop a skepticism about what was really the truth. I was a good communist, doing what I was supposed to do, and yet something nagged at me with this way of life."

"When I was younger," she says, "the government took care of the children. After-school programs, summer camps, and education was free. There were very few illiterate people."

She even had a music teacher from the Moscow Conservatory who gave her lessons twice a week. Her parents couldn't afford piano lessons, so she learned to play the accordion. Looking back, she realizes that the government did provide many opportunities for them.

Her father drove a truck for a chicken-farm company that provided equipment for those farms. Her mother worked in a government office. Every job was supported by the government. Life was predictable. For Marina, however, the seeds of rebellion were being sown.

She remembers that her parents were very hard workers and had a strong work ethic. Still, because her parents worked long hours, she often had to take care of herself. Her grandmother, with whom she was very close, died when she was eight years old. She was devastated, and she now was even more often alone.

A rebellious Marina fought with her father, especially disagreeing with his strict ways. He would also blame her for upsetting her mother and making her sick. The air of the household was often thick with anger.

When she was 15, she was one of the leaders in the local Communist Party youth organization. She recalls that nothing of significance really happened in those meetings other than the members routinely reinforcing the greatness of the Soviet Union.

The meetings were also a place where the older men in their twenties and thirties would sexually harass the younger girls. Marina was not personally affected, but she knew girls who were. There was no recourse for these offenses. This only added to her questions about the party's values.

Her mother gave her a subscription to a magazine called *Yunost* (Youth) that sometimes published controversial ideas outside of those promoted by the Soviet government. She began to ponder ideas related to freedom that were included in articles about America. She saw and understood things that her teachers would never discuss. It was uncommon for someone to have this magazine, but she quietly absorbed all of its contents, relishing the freedom of thought it offered her.

Born in 1974, she grew up during communist rule under Brezhnev, Mikhail Gorbachev, and Boris Yeltsin. It was Gorbachev, however, in 1985, who began *glasnost* (openness) and *perestroika* (restructuring). It was also a time of great confusion for the people of the soon-to-be-former Soviet Union.

"You must remember," she says, "that our lives were set up for us under communist rule. We knew we'd always have a place to live, food, and jobs, all courtesy of the government."

"We didn't know what to make of all that we had been told daily about the greatness of our country and the evils in the West. All that we had been taught about the communist system was being dismantled. It was all a big lie!"

Gorbachev saw that reforms were necessary because of the economic woes that were befalling the Soviet Union. He relaxed the bureaucracy and reduced censorship. Yet, despite this, his attempts at economic reforms largely failed.

Under his rule, the Cold War ostensibly ended. He met with President Ronald Reagan and forged a nuclear armistice. It was to Gorbachev that Reagan famously said in a speech to "tear down the [Berlin] Wall." By the time Gorbachev left office, the Wall had indeed been taken down, and some of the Soviet-bloc countries began to declare their independence, such as Ukraine, Belorussia, and Lithuania.

In 1991, reactionary hard-liners in the Communist Party, fearing the collapse of the Soviet Union, attempted to remove Gorbachev. He was imprisoned in his holiday home in Crimea. The military attempted to seize control of the Russian parliament, but, thwarted by the efforts of Russian President Boris Yeltsin and mass protests, the coup failed. Gorbachev returned to Moscow but soon realized that the balance of power and popular support had shifted to Yeltsin.

Yeltsin banned all Communist Party activities on Russian territory, and he signed a treaty with the presidents of Ukraine and Belorussia to create a new commonwealth of republics. Without these key nations, and given other political upheavals, the Soviet Union dissolved, and Gorbachev resigned.

Despite successfully ushering in a freer and more open society, Yeltsin's tenure from 1991 to 1999 was marred by economic hardship, increased corruption and crime, a violent war in the breakaway republic of Chechnya, and Russia's diminished influence on world events.

Poverty deepened during Yeltsin's reign. True, the country had a more democratic and capitalistic leaning, but the old Russian oligarchs managed to keep the wealth in their hands, leaving many struggling with a very unsteady economy.

In the early 1990s, Russian culture was altered from doing what "the Party" dictated to punk music, decadence, widespread economic decline, and confusion.

"Things changed practically overnight," Marina says. "Many of us didn't know what to do with this new-found freedom. We were forced to make a complete turn when Gorbachev took power, yet we didn't know how, or to what? And then along came Yeltsin, and the system that we had known and had been indoctrinated into was gone."

At the time, she was attending medical school but switched to nursing school and got her degree. She went into dermatology, realizing that she needed to make her own money to live independent of her parents.

After she left home and moved into her own apartment, her relationship with her parents changed for the better. Now the pressure was for her to get married. She did, but acknowledges that it was a bad idea. She was 18, and it lasted only six months.

"The men in my life while in Russia always wanted to stop my independent development. Typical of them in those days, they wanted to control women," she says.

She told her mother that she would not marry another Russian man, have children with one, or endure the way that most of them treated their wives and girlfriends. For emphasis she characterizes a typical Russian man at the time with this: "What's for dinner? I am going on a trip, pack my suitcase. Do this, do that!" She does acknowledge that today the younger generation of men are different: they are learning to understand how to treat women better, and women are learning to understand how to be treated as equal partners.

By the time Yeltsin assumed the presidency, and even with a freer republic, Marina knew that what had been churning inside her since her days in the Communist Party — the doubt about the veracity of what she was told since she was very young, and the nagging feeling that blossomed in her late teens and early twenties — meant that Russia was not the place for her. Her values were very different.

She certainly knew many others who agreed with her that the Soviet Union, and subsequently Russia, promoted a mentality of cynicism over the promises made by the government, but it also was steeped in misogyny, homophobia, and antisemitism that persisted among many of its citizens.

A friend of hers told her about an agency called Life Partner, a sort of Russo-American Match.com that arranged meetings for potential marriage between American men and Russian women. Marina dismissed this at first, but her friend convinced her to give it a try, which she did. This was at the end of 1996.

The following spring, she met Joe through the agency, and a month later — though she knew just a little English and had never been out of Russia — she left for the United States; she and Joe married in 1998. They then moved to Northern California.

Marina felt safe with Joe. This was a strange and perhaps even risky situation, but with him she was comfortable. She liked him from the start. She loves him to this day.

During her first year in California, however, she was emotionally distraught, homesick for her family and her country. Joe didn't know what to do to help her. With his encouragement, Marina returned to Russia. She didn't know if she would go back to Joe. She wrestled with many factors during an emotional and turbulent time for her.

During those weeks in Russia, her parents welcomed her return. They now treated her with respect and kindness. There were so many things she had missed in Russia. Still, though the country had changed in many ways, it was still under a repressive government led by Vladimir Putin.

After having been home for eight weeks, Marina came to the realization that she needed to be with Joe and to make a life for herself and her new husband in California. He was unsure if she would return, he would later tell her, but had hoped she would. He was scared, she says. But she knew that she had to go back to him.

She returned to the United States, never looking back again. She visits every year and relishes those times. She misses it; the culture is still a strong part of who she is. Her three daughters, one in college, one in high school, and one in middle school, all speak Russian and celebrate their mother's culture, which brings a gleam to her eyes.

She has reached her goal of becoming a registered nurse in the United States, and she wishes someday to return to school in midwifery. She and Joe have been married for twenty years, and she is content with her decision to become a U.S. citizen.

Marina gets a wistful look as she tells me of a documentary film that she and Joe saw in a small theater in San Francisco. Called *My Perestroika*, it follows the lives of four different people who live under

Putin now but who reflect back on what their lives had been like as children, and how it compares to today. She cried throughout the movie, telling me that "this was my life, my story!"

Does she miss Russia? She becomes nostalgic talking about it. The beauty of her village, her family, and her friends. However, this is her home. This is the place she's chosen to live. This is the country that gives her and her family opportunities that they could not have in Russia. She is an American-Russian; that is who she wants to be.

Yugoslavia, in the 1980s following President Tito's death, began to unravel. The Balkans War, as it was known, lasted from 1991 to 1999, with each of six regions of Yugoslavia seeking independence. Thousands upon thousands were killed and displaced. Serbs sought to rid the region of Bosnian Muslims and Croats under the harsh reign of Radovan Karadzic. UN peacekeepers had limited success in stopping the war. Many suffered, and the story of one Muslim family sheds light on the trauma that many endured, but for them their journey eventually led to finding safety in the United States.

For centuries, the multi-ethnic region that was home to Mirela and her family was a peaceful place. For Bosnian Muslims, who are different from Arabic Muslims in many ways, their Christian and Jewish neighbors were all part of the communities that all lived in. In the years that followed Tito's death, those communities began to fall apart as politicians try to capitalize on divisiveness and fear.

Mirela

In 1991, Bosanski Novi in Bosnia was a small city of 28,000; on a hillside above was a small enclave called Izba, which by foot meant a half-mile walk down to get to the center of the city. These places are situated in the Kula Mountain Range bordering Croatia. Although Sabi was from the city below, after she and

Fikret got married they moved to where he had lived in Izba, which had only 32 households. In their modest home, they lived downstairs, and Fikret's brother, his brother's wife, and their two children, along with his mother, lived upstairs.

They loved their little village, as they referred to it. This was a close-knit community where people took care of one another. Their daughter, Mirela, describes how she and her younger brother and younger sister would play with friends on the grassy hillsides nearby. Playfully racing through the fields dotted with its brilliant wild flowers, or sledding down the snowy hills in winter, brings a smile to her face as she relishes the vivid memory.

There was no running water in Izba, and Sabi would retrieve it from a nearby river for drinking, cooking, and cleaning. Before winter, the people would chop wood to prepare for the cold and snow that would engulf the region. All this was an accepted part of life that kindled the spirits of the hardy hillside people.

Fikret would walk down to Bosanski Novi to the import/export business where he worked for five years before the war that broke apart Yugoslavia, a war that would change their lives forever. Prior to that, he had done odd jobs just to bring in some money. Mirela says he was a stubborn, proud man who would do anything rather than ask for financial help, so the family was somewhat relieved when he got the job at the import/export business.

Mirela's family would venture to the city below for groceries, and other goods, and to visit relatives. Also, the mosques and schools were in the city, so the half-mile was done as routinely as any daily task. Mirela remembers her life to be an idyllic existence consisting of her hilltop enclave, other similar villages in the mountains, and the beautiful buildings built long ago in the city below.

Established in 1280 in a location that is now northwestern Bosnia and Herzegovina, Bosanski Novi got its name in 1895. There was a wooden bridge system built to provide escape from the often-occurring spring and fall floods by the Una and Sana Rivers. In 1872, it became the first Bosnian municipality to have its own railway station. This allowed for the flow of cultural and economic advantages.

The region later became part of Yugoslavia and was inhabited by many Muslims, both practicing and non-practicing. In the early 1980s, something sinister was brewing, and the effects on Bosnia's Muslim population, and on Mirela's family in particular, would be devastating.

Most older Muslim women in that region would wear hijabs only during holy days. At that time, and even today, Fikret continues to be a more adherent follower of Islam than the rest of his family, who are considered non-practicing although they attend services at their local mosque on holy days.

After Tito, the president of Yugoslavia, died in 1982, the separation of religions in that country began to take hold as politicians would preach the perceived evils of each. Christians and Muslims were beginning to align within their own ethnic and religious divides. Bosanski Novi was multicultural, and the schisms there had never truly developed despite what was beginning to take shape elsewhere. That is, until 1991.

By the middle of 1991, groups within Bosanski Novi began to fervently associate with their religion and their ethnicity. Serbs, Croats, and Bosnians all claimed that they were the rightful inhabitants of the land and that they were willing to fight for it. Even in this small city, divisiveness encroached on what had been a peaceful coexistence.

Fikret recalls that the Muslims in his village and in Bosanski Novi had no weapons. However, in mid-1991 the Serbs, who were fighting among themselves for power and control, blamed the Muslims for the violence. The atmosphere was fouled with the stench of hate, and the region's Muslims were beginning to feel the intensity of Serbian wrath.

Serbs, who took control of the local governments in all of the small towns and cities in the region, had established a curfew where no one could venture outside from 8:00 p.m. to 6:00 a.m. Serbian flags appeared on municipal buildings and police stations.

Fikret relays a story about a neighbor of theirs who went out to have a cigarette after curfew, and a sniper killed him. Bosnian citizens in other villages and cities, too, were literally now in the line of fire as the Serbian fear campaign took hold.

According to Fikret, the Serbs were now seen randomly entering villages, killing people, and then returning to their posts in the cities.

Izba's residents set up a "neighborhood watch" system to alert the others, but what could they actually do? They had no weapons, nor did they want to fight.

The Serbs were in control of the area and would have undoubtedly overpowered the Bosnian Muslims.

Sabi interjects that, following the murder of their neighbor, the villagers were in a constant state of anxiety. Since Izba bordered Croatia, they could see that those villages were burning at the hands of the Serbs. Children of Izba were constantly crying. Sleep was not easy for anyone. An escalation of Serbian aggression was building.

Mirela recalls that, at age 6, she was a rebellious child and she resisted going down for a nap like her mother wanted for her and her siblings. She overheard her parents saying that a war was coming and that they needed a plan. She tearfully remembers her dad saying that he'd put a VCR player and some clothes in a bag for Sabi to sell in case he was killed.

The intimidation tactics being used by the Serbs included sending in some of their own to tell the villagers to run and hide in the woods because the "bad" Serbs would soon come to kill them. Trust, belief, and equilibrium now damaged, the Bosnians were unsure of what to do.

In broken English, Sabi describes how everyone in the village decided that sleeping in one house was their only option. The unarmed men stood by the doors to provide what little protection they could. She recalls that, for three months, they lived like this. "No one will come here to kill my kids!" she says with the strength that comes from a mother willing to die to protect her children.

In Bosanski Novi down below, the mosques and other buildings were being burned. The smell of smoke rose along with the fear. Gunfire from Serbian weapons replaced what were once the sounds of a normal, thriving city.

"During momentary pauses in the shooting, the Serbs sent their fighters to tell the villagers that they needed to surrender. This moment in 1992 began the end of our village," says Mirela.

They exited with a white flag, and all the inhabitants of Izba marched downhill while the Serbs shot into the air, each sound bringing a tear to their captives.

"We were brought to the local high school," says Mirela, "which served as a concentration camp. There was no food, no water. It was stifling hot, and the oppression was unbearable. We wept while our parents did what they could to comfort us. Shhh my darling, the mothers would utter, as if to calm a child from a scraped knee."

"Four villages were crammed into the building. We were given moldy bread once in the morning. My father distributed it," remembers Mirela, "but he didn't give any to his family. In his mind, he couldn't see us taking it from others who might be in more need. My uncle said he'd rather see the kids get the bread, and he refused his share. He gave us his portion."

Sabi and Fikret echo that they were not frightened for their own lives but for those of the kids. "If we die we die," says Sabi, "but please let our kids live."

While the Muslim villagers were in the concentration camp, their captors promised that they would live this time; they claimed their houses were just being checked to make sure there were no weapons or plans to deter the Serbs. The Serbs then gave permission to ten male prisoners to check on the houses, and Fikret was one of them. This was done, they said, to show the beneficence of the soldiers and to prove that nothing was taken or destroyed in their homes. To the men's surprise, little had changed in

Izba. The following day, all of the prisoners were allowed leave the camp and go home.

Their time in the camp had lasted four days. They were in stifling hot and airless confines, wearing the same clothes, with little access to water and sanitation, and no understanding of what would happen to them, until the Serbs finally freed them.

The villagers' fear and the Serbian intimidation tactics persisted, however. The day the villagers were released, the Serbs announced in their newspapers that ten terrorists had tried to invade homes in Izba but that the Serbs had protected the villagers from these marauders.

As part of the propaganda arm of their assault on Bosnia, the Serbs wanted to show the people how critical it was for Serbian soldiers to be present to prevent terrorist activity. Of course, the Bosnians did not believe them, but the news went beyond the tiny villages and cities, and out to news outlets and governments around the world.

Following the villagers' release, the Serbs ordered the men to go back to work and the families to live their lives as if nothing had changed. However, the anguish and pain suffered by Mirela, her family, the people of Izba, and their fellow Bosnian Muslims were irreparable. They moved their bodies as if in a dream, a nightmare really. There was no normalcy in this hell.

"We were scavenging for food. There was a little bit of oil and flour for bread, but not much else. My parents always put on a brave face for us children," recalls Mirela somewhat wistfully.

Two and a half weeks after the first march to the concentration camp, they were rounded up again. This time, mostly women and children joined 6,000 in the city's soccer stadium. Fikret and many of the other men were taken to another place, where they were psychologically tortured and tormented.

Sabi recalls that, this time, things got worse and that a deeper, even more searing kind of horror had emerged. Her eyes tear up as the memory seems to reluctantly surface.

They shared a bitter memory of being marched to the soccer stadium, which held 6,000 Bosnian Muslims. They look in one another's eyes, revealing a silent and solemn connection between mother and daughter, while Mirela describes the horror of the events that unfolded.

"I remember this muscular soldier wearing a huge crucifix sitting atop a tank who yelled orders to both crawl, and then walk," Mirela continues. "My grandma was too frail, but had to follow his orders." She chuckles now at the image of her grandmother crawling when everyone was upright, and being upright when all others were crawling. She just couldn't keep up.

"Then the muscled soldier shot my little cousins who were holding hands through the forearm of one of them; it went right through her! The other bullet just grazed the arm of the other [cousin]. The Serbs took my little cousin who was bleeding and screaming in pain, but we didn't know where. My mom was so upset with what we were seeing that she tried to drag us children into the river that we were walking next to, saying that it's better we all drown than to be at the mercy of the Serbs."

Mirela doesn't know how it was they didn't drown. It was chaotic and frightening, but eventually they arrived at the stadium.

"You go there, the armed soldiers would shout, YOU THERE! Shut your kids up from crying or I'll kill them, and you will watch, and then I'll kill you."

There was hardly any food or water. Sleep was not to be had. The sounds of anguish from the children was deafening. The cruelty of the soldiers was maddening. The horror of what was happening was incomprehensible.

Mirela says, "since my mom's parents lived on the outskirts of the city, they were left alone by the Serbs and not taken to the concentration camp for some reason."

Her grandfather visited the camp, and, when "he held up three fingers, the symbol of the Serbs, and a white flag," he was allowed to enter. He wandered through the stadium calling out my mom's name and the names of her two brothers. He had brought us food hidden in his coat. We were starving, but so thankful for his bravery."

After enduring the indignation and suffering in this camp, they were inexplicably allowed to leave after a week.

Upon their release, a friend of Fikret gave Sabi a key to his apartment, so that Sabi and her two children, along with Fikret's mother, brother, and his family, could hide. They were told by the Serbs to go wherever they wanted, but not to be on the streets after curfew.

"Not knowing where my dad was, or my wounded cousin, we found our way to the safety of the friend's apartment. We needed time to pause, to think, to understand what had befallen us, and to figure out how to survive," says Mirela.

Mirela recalls that one day her uncle frantically screamed at them to hide; a Serbian soldier was coming. It was actually Fikret, who had been given a Yugoslavian uniform when he was released from his concentration camp because his other clothing was in tatters.

Mirela recalls, "we were overcome with joy. We all raced over to him like little puppies greeting their mother. The joy was short-lived as the realities of our lives came back into focus."

"My sister was very dehydrated, so my father took her to the local hospital. His uniform and his beard fooled the Serbs. I recall that the Serbs with long beards were more murderous. They would kill whoever they saw that was not Serb. My father's beard was short, but it showed, at least to the Serbs, that he was one of them. His disguise worked."

At the hospital, Fikret lied to the workers that he was a Serbian soldier, so they gave his daughter intravenous saline to treat her dehydration. He brought her back to the apartment, but then was told by his brother that his little girl had been shot through her arm. Fikret raced back to the hospital and found his niece lying untreated in a dingy hospital room. He wrested her from her bed and they quickly exited, returning to the tiny apartment where his family was in hiding.

The next day they learned that all of the Bosnian Muslim patients in the hospital had been executed by the Serbs.

After a week in the apartment, the family returned to their home in the village, one of the few structures not burned down. But the Serbs now made anyone still remaining to sign their home over to them, and in exchange the families were given money to purchase bus tickets to leave the city.

Mirela recalls, "the bus took us 30 kilometers from Izba. The Serbs then stopped the bus, and their plan to kill us was revealed. They had done the same to all Bosnian Muslims from our region. They would send the bus over the Croatian border and execute everyone before throwing them into mass graves, we learned."

What ensued was nothing less than miraculous. The United Nations had stationed their peace-keepers on that border who now understood what was transpiring. They stopped the buses from crossing the border.

Mirela says, "they sent us back to Izba at midnight. It was empty; a ghost town. There was no one and nothing left. We slept at one of my father's friends' house. The next day, megaphones blared that our worries were over, that curfew was over, and that we were going to go to new countries. We couldn't believe them, but we had no choice, and we were confused and exhausted."

"We were all put into UN trucks, and ferried to a refugee camp in Croatia. They were protecting us from the Serbs. There we stayed in a school that had been converted to a holding place for the many of us who had been saved from the unfolding genocide. We slept on cots, were given food and water, slowly began to awaken from the nightmare that had been our lives for the past several months," Mirela says.

She further remembers that "it was luck that we ran into the Red Cross at that camp that assigned us to be on a train to Germany. We were one of the first that actually got to leave. We didn't know where we were going, and we didn't know where any of our relatives were, but we knew we were leaving the Serbian atrocities behind."

The sense of relief is shared among Mirela, Fikret, and Sabi as they describe how they could finally sleep and feel safe. On the train were Red Cross workers, doctors, nurses, and other personnel, which gave them the security to know that this was not a dream.

They were delivered to a refugee camp in Muenster, Germany, where they were taken care of for a month before being moved to Dusseldorf in August 1992. This was when the full force of the war in Bosnia began.

"I remember watching the German news, which was uncensored, seeing torture and beheadings of our countrymen," Mirela says. "Our hearts ached for what was taking place. With full knowledge of what was happening, the world stopped short of intervening in the genocide of the Bosnian Muslims."

"On a positive note, my father, who volunteered to help in the war relief efforts, found out where all of our relatives were in Germany."

Mirela loved Germany, and the feeling of safety and freedom. She had friends in school, too, and a new-found calm had finally arrived.

They were in an apartment building living in two rooms with a separate bathroom. German social services provided for their needs, and the children went to school. In 2002, Fikret's mother wanted to be with her other son who had moved to the United States after being sponsored by Catholic Charities of Central New York in 1999. He sent them the paperwork to sponsor their journey toward citizenship in the U.S., and after six months they headed for America.

Mirela had not cut her hair for years, but in a rebellious act in protest of the move to Utica, New York, she reduced it to a mere bob.

"I had found peace in Germany. I was 16, and wanted to stay."

In Utica, there were no buses, trains, and high rises like in Germany.

"I was scared," Mirela says. "The change was enormous for us. Still, my father gave us three months to learn English. He is a very determined man, and he wanted us to fit into our new life in the U.S. The refugee center provided the English lessons and other services, so we learned to speak English as best as we could."

"I was a junior in high school and was trying to figure out how to become American. I learned both German while in Germany, and English while here from the TV show, 'The Nanny.' Can you imagine, Fran Drescher and her cohorts taught me to speak two languages that were otherwise foreign to me?"

In Germany, she hadn't talked about the war. In Utica, the other Bosnian students, who were Muslim too, wanted to know what political party she was affiliated with. Even now, twenty-three years after the war ended, the Bosnians butt heads over political divisions. It wasn't a particularly welcoming scenario, to say the least. The memories that were opened up by these unpleasant conversations were ones that she preferred to have left behind in Bosnia.

Mirela pauses for a moment, then adds, "my opinion is that the war happened; women were raped, parents separated from each other and their kids, children killed, and homes destroyed. Our political leaders were in their villas enjoying life while all of this went on. I cannot trust most politicians. My father disagrees with me. He says we need to have faith in those who truly want what's best for the people. I am not quite ready to adhere to that dogma."

"I married an American, have two beautiful American-born sons, and have a number of American friends, but it is hard for them to understand what it means to survive a war. We came to this country, though not my choice, to escape the horror of that war. Had this never happened to us we would still be in Izba."

"I see what is happening to refugees and those needing safe haven today, and it breaks my heart. Their stories, like ours, need to be told. Their anguish needs to be salved. This world needs to heal."

In a wistful moment, the three of them gently hug me goodbye.

The Yugoslav Wars, which occurred from 1991 to 2001, were actually a series of separate conflicts resulting in the formation of independent republics. These were ethnic conflicts, insurgencies, and wars of independence. However, the increased influence of the Serbian government under the rule of Slobodan Milosevic, whose aim it was to create a "Greater Serbia" to include parts of Croatia and Bosnia, loomed large throughout the entire decade. At war's end, Milosevic and others were convicted of war crimes including genocide, crimes against humanity, and rape perpetrated against Bosnian Muslims.

Dina

Until the age of nine, Dina, her younger brother, Kemal, her parents, Naser and Lida, and their extended family lived a middle-class life in Donji Vakuf, a town in central Bosnia. She loved learning, and school was an important component of her life. However, when the country, formerly known as Yugoslavia, broke out in wars fueled by ethnic conflict, things changed drastically for her. Her neighborhood was no longer safe, and it became obvious that things were getting dangerous in the country. Life as she knew it was about to take a drastic turn.

"As kids, we could no longer play freely as it wasn't as safe anymore. School days became shorter and shorter until we finally didn't go to school," she says as she reflects on the changes that had begun to take hold.

Going back several generations, Dina's Muslim family had been farmers in Bosnia. Her parents were from Donji Vakuf but her grandparents were not. Her grandmother on her mother's side was from a different city, and so was her grandfather on her father's side. This was a fairly normal course for many who lived in the region.

Her paternal grandparents had met while her grandfather was a soldier in the Yugoslav army. He subsequently became the chief of police in her town, where he earned a great deal of respect for his honesty and fairness. Dina's other grandfather worked at a local lumber company. The family was close-knit, worked hard, and genuinely celebrated life together.

Dina's father, who had always been wary of Yugoslav president Tito, who died in 1980, was no less wary of the turmoil that was brewing in Bosnia. In March 1993, having heard stories of the Serbian government's targeting of Muslims in Bosnia, Naser took his family including his mother-in-law, and other women relatives, to Croatia. They hastily made their way. Dina only brought one childhood item with her.

"It's funny", says Dina, "but I was never really into dolls. I liked marbles, cars, and trucks, but I took one doll that had been given to me by aunt. I suppose it was important because it represented a little part of me, my home, and my country."

With a wistful sigh, she admits that it also represented a peaceful and loving time in her life.

Dina's grandfathers and uncles stayed behind, wanting to protect their property. Little did they know that, a month after their family had departed for Croatia, they would be killed by invading Serbs. The awful truth that her father had feared had actually been set into motion, with the resulting tragedy that befell the men who stayed behind.

It was not until several years later that her family learned of this truth. They were left with overwhelming sadness and grief, but also with questions of who was responsible and what could be done to seek justice.

While in Croatia, they didn't engage in many activities — it was a life of uncertainty, of an unfamiliarity as to how to live, incredulous at what was left behind, and not knowing what was ahead.

Still, Dina says, they were lucky. They got an apartment that had belonged to a family that moved out. Including extended family, seven of them lived in one room. This was cramped quarters, but only temporary, they thought. And they were out of the line of fire from the Serbs. Other refugees lived in rundown wooden barracks, which she describes as almost like an abandoned Boy Scout camp in the forest.

During that time, Dina started attending school in a somewhat decrepit building that provided her with an accelerated version of education. Her third grade was completed in roughly a month. The education provided was a collaboration between the Croatian government and the refugees there who had been teachers in Bosnia.

During the summer, she recalls going to the ocean to dig for seashells and pass the time on the beach. However, this was much less idyllic than one might assume. There was lots of idle time, and always the hope of returning home. Throughout her stay in Croatia, her parents would read the newspapers or watch the TV news to see if the war was over so they could leave. That never came.

Dina recalls, "We'd spend days playing and waiting for the day that we would hear the news to go back to Bosnia. My family was in Croatia for about eight months. It was during this time that conflict broke out between Bosnia and Croatia, and we were given twenty-four hours to leave [Croatia]. Going home was once again not going to be in our reality."

"As a child, I remember feeling anxious and afraid of what was waiting for us. I remember [wondering] whether my aunt and uncle [would come] with us, but they didn't. They didn't because they had resident status in Croatia and they were not told to leave like we were. Once again, we were being separated from our extended family."

The number of Bosnians fleeing to neighboring Croatia had grown to a humanitarian crisis in relation to housing as well as food supply. It became abundantly clear that much of the world had turned a blind eye to what was happening. However, the Pakistani government stepped in to help the Bosnians by bringing many to refugee camps in its country. In 1993, that is where Dina and her family headed.

She describes the transition as another dizzying episode in her young life.

"We fled Bosnia to live in rundown houses in Croatia, but war there required us to leave again. Pakistan was kind enough to take us in, but the culture was so different from ours it was difficult to assimilate."

They lived with three other families in a large, abandoned building with concertina wire all around. For a year they all shared a small room, with limited kitchen and bathroom space. The lack of privacy was constant. Pakistan, though a beautiful country, was a very different environment. It was hot, humid, and for the most part dirty in the city where the refugee camp was.

"We could not leave the camp without police escort as it was not deemed safe for us because we were European. The food was very difficult to get used to. At first, the government fed us three meals a day, but then, after they realized that we could not get used to it, they proceeded to give us an allowance and sponsor trips to Islamabad to buy groceries. After this, we made our own familiar meals," she says.

"I was in a dream, more like a nightmare, having gone through what we did. Now I was eleven years old, in an unfamiliar place, not knowing what the future held."

A year later, they were placed in a single-family unit in the building, and, though it was still unsettling, having their own apartment was much better.

As she continued to anchor herself in school, Dina found that the education provided in Pakistan for the Bosnians was quite good. She learned some English and absorbed the subject matter being taught. The rest of Dina's family, like all of the refugees, had a hard time getting used to their camp environment. Both of her parents were working adults back in Bosnia, but in Pakistan there was no work. The adults stayed in the rooms all day and played cards and chess and waited for news from Bosnia on the status of the war.

The need and desire to work was constant with most Bosnian adults in the refugee camp. They just couldn't get used to a life without it. "

She remembers the emotions that those in the camp exhibited.

"The adults, including my parents, were very anxious but also felt helpless as they were thousands of miles away from Bosnia. Every day we awaited news and word that the war had ended so that we could go back home and continue living our lives in our own country. This day didn't come. The adults idled, which had a negative effect on some of their relationships, so we started seeing divisions in the refugee camp. Some adults were for staying in Pakistan and others were for setting wheels in motion to move to another country. Perhaps America?"

While in Pakistan, and at the age of eleven, Dina met a woman named Julie Mertus who, along with a team of human rights researchers, had visited the refugee camps and some homes around the world to learn of the lives of fleeing Bosnians and Croatians. Julie's book, The Suitcase: Refugee Voices from Bosnia and Croatia, was published in 1997.

"She interviewed my family and we ended up in her book," Dina says.

She remembers thinking that "this is who I want to be like someday." Julie was smart, respectful (wearing a hijab though she was not Muslim), and caring. The impression she made on young Dina would be lasting in her own professional pursuits as she grew older.

Several Bosnian families eventually found their way to the United States. A small enclave formed in

Utica, New York. Dina had a relative there who sponsored them, and in 1995 they were able to get the documentation to leave.

She recalls the rawness of the departure.

"Departing Pakistan, once again, produced anxiety. Where are we going now? What awaits? Who will be there to greet us? The travel time was long. Long and exhausting. I remember thinking as a little girl that America will feel more like Bosnia. I am not sure why I had this view or where it came from, but there was one thing I did know for sure: there was snow!"

Dina continues, "Initially, life in Utica was very difficult. Another start, new country, new system, new language, new everything. The first year or so we spent just surviving, gathering other people's discards and donations, including furniture, shoes, and toys."

School was hard because Dina spoke British English, which she had learned in Pakistan. She was picked on and bullied, which made it difficult to love school and to feel a sense of belonging. As the years went on, the bullying subsided, and the adjustment to her new home took hold.

When the war in her former country ended in 2001, much pain and grief had to be reconciled for the surviving families, many of whom were now part of the diaspora of Bosnian Muslims who had moved to other parts of the world. For Dina and her family, finding out the details about her grandfathers' deaths would be important.

In 2003, a United Nations–sponsored program to identify relatives killed in the war contacted Dina's family and requested that they go to Bosnia to claim the remains of her grandfathers. In 2005, she and her parents made the trek back to what was only a horrific memory of their former country.

"It was another surreal journey that left us all with an empty feeling. Although one would like to find closure at that point, it merely left us deeply hurt and angry," she remembers.

Through DNA sampling from Dina and family, the U.N. program was able to make a match. The remains of her paternal grandfather were just skeletal bones. Dina recalls how awful she felt and the bitterness that now surfaced. It was a difficult return, to be sure.

In 2007, the U.N. contacted her family again to identify her other grandfather's remains. Her parents went, but Dina could not bear to go back again.

Dina has her master's degree in sociology and a PhD in social psychology. She is a professor at a local college in Utica. She attributes her interest in these areas because of what she went through. However, she is still dumbfounded at how people can be so evil and cruel as she experienced with the war in Bosnia.

"I studied these academic areas to try to get a better handle on the many ways that humans behave and to see how we can intervene, and yet to this day those who tend toward cruelty still exist," she says.

"And yet my boss always comments that I have an amazing zest for life."

He is right about that, she says; despite what she has experienced, or likely because of it, her hope and faith in people abounds.

She reflects that, when she sees some of her students today who are going through something similar to what she experienced, she clearly empathizes despite the sadness that it brings her.

"Some of what I see going on in the world today breaks my heart. As an immigrant, I sometimes have felt like an intruder. As a refugee, I see that as Americans we are extremely welcoming. We are built on diversity. I understand that we have to be careful as a nation by vetting those who come in, but Islamophobia and xenophobia have spread worldwide and are clearly on the rise. Sadly, we shut doors to people because of a label or false perceptions."

"For me personally, I don't look stereotypically Muslim. I don't adhere a lot of the practices though some in my family do; I am lighter skinned; and I don't wear a hijab. Yet when some learn that I am Muslim, the air in the room can literally change. Still, I do feel lucky to be in America. We are able to disagree with our government and say so publicly without fear. There are many countries where this is not possible. This is the beauty of living in this democracy."

Dina, her husband (who is from Bosnia as well), and their young daughter enjoy the lives they have carved out in America. They travel freely and have seen many parts of this country and have gone abroad.

Her life was forever altered by her experiences as a child, and those experiences remain a guiding force in her work, including research she is doing on Bosnian war victims. She believes her path as an adult was chosen for her as a child enduring the cruelty that came hurtling at her but also encountering the kindness that existed. She now uses those harsh lessons to help make the world a more peaceful and enduring place for others.

Armenian Christians were long persecuted within the Ottoman Empire (later known as Turkey), but in 1915 the prejudice took a very violent turn, leading to what is known today as the Armenian Genocide. Of the two million Armenians who had lived in the Empire, by 1922 only 388,000 survived. Thousands of them escaped to other countries.

A small Armenian community formed in Addis Ababa, Ethiopia. Its members brought new skills and expertise to the small African nation. Armenians had a long history of trade with Ethiopia, which was primarily a Christian nation, so it became a haven for those fleeing the terror in Turkey.

Avo

Of Armenian Christian descent, but born in Ethiopia because his grandparents established roots there after fleeing to Russia and Syria during the genocide in the Ottoman Empire, Avo's story begins. Much of his family walked the hundreds of miles to these countries. Some died along the way. His father's side of the family ended up in France; his mother's family lived for a time in Syria; eventually, most of them moved to Addis Ababa. The trauma that was perpetrated on his family still brings about a sadness in

Avo but also a sense of pride that they overcame those horrors through determination and faith.

His parents met in Africa and married in 1945. He was born in Addis Ababa in 1955, the second of four children. His grandparents were influential in his life; in particular, his paternal grandmother was very open and eager to retell the stories of her survival. To this day, he says, when he meets other immigrants, he senses what he calls "the survival instinct" as was experienced by his grandmother.

She told him that their lives were seen as having no value in the Ottoman Empire. "But she didn't teach me hatred. She was telling me that this is what happened to them, but that the Armenian culture survived and would be passed on to subsequent generations."

There was no country that stepped forward to rescue his grandparents and other Armenians. It was World War I, and the world was in chaos. Reestablishing order in the whole of Europe was the objective on the part of the allies at that time.

"We Armenians become contributors to any country we go to. In Ethiopia we were part of the community that included all religions. We had a good life. No fear of walking the streets, going to school, or playing in our neighborhood," says Avo.

He went to a French school and learned many languages and about many cultures. It was an important upbringing for him, which would later pay off.

Avo attended church regularly with his grandmother. She would talk to him about the importance of community and of not focusing on material items. She was reluctant to talk about the atrocities of her own experiences in Turkey, concentrating instead on how she and others survived the exodus itself. Still, she instilled a faith in humanity that, despite her own past, stays with Avo to this day.

For many years, he enjoyed his life in Ethiopia. The multiculturalism added to the richness of his community. His teachers were a great influence on how to view that community and value all that it offered.

And yet the unspoken but ever-presence of one thing remained: he grew up as "Armenian Stateless." As much as they loved their lives in

Ethiopia, they were still "foreigners" in this country. They didn't have passports. It bothered him that this status was their identity; it was even recorded as such in the government census.

He also learned of some of the cultural realities of his day through the experiences of his classmates in Ethiopia. He recalls that some of the Israeli students were called back to Israel during the Six Day War in 1967. It unnerved him that teens would be called back to their countries to fight in a war. Other classmates from Eastern Europe defected to West European countries.

Growing up in an upper-middle-class family in Ethiopia, Avo's family had maids, which was the norm for many families. He always felt comfortable but never thought of himself as privileged. Regardless of skin color, he was taught — in his family as well as at school — that equality was paramount. Ethiopians were "god-fearing people," and their Christian teachings were important to the mindset he was developing.

It was the political turmoil of the late 1960s and early 1970s that further altered the lives of Avo and his family.

Haile Selassie, the long-time "emperor" of Ethiopia, was deposed by coup in 1974. Under his rule, many in Ethiopia had good lives. He was a benevolent leader who was perceived as caring for his people. During his 44-year reign, he pledged to promote economic, social, and educational reforms. Though in exile for five years after the invasion of his country by Italy in 1936, he returned with assistance from Great Britain in 1941, at which time his reforms resumed until the great famine of 1974 that brought down his government.

In the late 1940s and early 1960s, Avo's two uncles had immigrated to New York from Ethiopia. The process was easy back then, and they became U.S. citizens. The older of the two joined the Army at age 18 and even fought in the Korean War. The younger uncle immigrated with his family. After starting a business (which ended up failing), he joined Motorola in Austin, Texas, where he worked for the rest of his career.

Avo's father, who was the oldest son, stayed in Ethiopia to ensure that his mother was taken care of. This was the grandmother with whom Avo became close. He didn't know his mother's parents well because they died when he was young. After grieving his paternal grandmother's death in 1970, Avo's family began the process of applying for immigration to the United States, where they had longed wished to go.

However, the revolution in Ethiopia was beginning, and it was difficult to leave. The government was now being exposed for its corruption, and more dictatorial tendencies emerged from Selassie. But it was the famine that ultimately triggered wide-spread anti-government activity.

When university students protested, the government's response was violent suppression. Avo recalls that his family didn't yet feel at-risk, and they had faith that things would be worked out.

However, Avo started to notice "the haves and the have nots" by the increasing homelessness that emerged around Addis Ababa. Though the famine didn't affect them personally, there was a very unsettled feeling that was now permeating their lives.

Eritrea, which had been in a federation with Ethiopia, was rebelling against Selassie in the

1960s after he demoted Eritrea to a province. This unrest, among other turbulence, was a warning to Avo's family that things were not going in the right direction.

The military in Ethiopia began to arrest the most corrupt government officials. Even soldiers were beginning to go hungry. Things were unraveling.

Avo's family started to worry about their safety and the stability of the government. They feared that Armenians might once again be targeted and victimized.

The Armenian Christians were by and large considered successful. As history has shown, it is often those who are seen as thriving that become scapegoated to benefit nationalist ideology. This was certainly on the minds of the Armenians in Ethiopia once again.

In mid-1974, a curfew was issued for the residents of the city, and those in the streets were now in jeopardy of being arrested, or worse. Avo was nineteen at the time, and his parents were especially worried about him as he was a bit oblivious to his surroundings.

"One day I went home after going on a date. My mother asked me if I had seen anything, and I said no. Well, she said, 60 high-ranking government officials were executed that night. It was at that time that reality set in," he recalls.

His sister had already gone to the United States, but he, his two other siblings, and his parents remained.

Finally, Selassie was stripped of his government and was imprisoned. This shocked most of Ethiopia, according to Avo; Salassie was seen as a leader who had mostly done good for his people.

Eventually, a military leader took over. Selassie died in prison, likely of starvation. The emperor's body was eventually discovered buried under a toilet after many months of not knowing what happened to it. Upon discovering this, Avo states, "we knew we had to leave."

The new government nationalized businesses and banks. They took over people's homes and put poor people in them. Non-Ethiopian people began to leave the country.

"We were not worried that we would be targeted. We were in a rented house, and it had already been nationalized, so ours couldn't be taken over. However, the curfew dictated our lives; freedom of movement was lost, and despair was setting in."

Moreover, the immigration process that my father had begun years before had slowed. Before approval, they needed background checks, Interpol clearance, and other documents that the U.S. government had now imposed. The wait was torturous.

Being "Armenian Stateless" complicated things. They had no passports, which made the process quite difficult. There was a consulate official who, after many years of the application process, told them she had "lost our paperwork." As he recounts this, Avo is clearly pained. After a long wait for approval, his family was to be back at square one.

"It was clear that she didn't like us, but we could not fathom why. Were we being targeted? Had we done something to offend her? This was in

1975 and we wanted out. We didn't know what to do," he says.

"As luck would have it, my two best friends had fathers who worked at the U.S. embassy. I spoke with both of them. One said he couldn't do anything, that he had no authority. But the other friend's father did have the authority to do something."

The friend's father learned that the consular agent had destroyed their papers. He had her removed from her duties. He put in a new consular agent whom he told to redo the process, and to expedite it. Then, Avo's friend and his family moved back to Maryland.

In the meantime, Avo's uncle in America did not respond to a request for documentation to provide financial support, as deemed necessary to sponsor the family's immigration. One day, however, to their surprise, the consular agent called them to sign the documents to grant them permission to leave.

Through tears, Avo describes the scene. "The agent told us that we had that gentleman to thank. He was referring to my friend's father. He said that he would take financial responsibility for us in the States as a sponsor should we need the help. It was a true miracle. We would not have been able to leave if not for him."

Avo's family moved to North Carolina to be with his sister for a few months. The gift of immigration had an enormous impact on him, of course. The realization that this man, who he only knew peripherally when he was visiting his friend, would do such a thing for him and his family, was hard to wrap his head around. He decided to take a bus to Maryland to personally thank the man for his act of true kindness.

"When I went to visit with them we celebrated Thanksgiving. He took me to the Great Catholic Cathedral in Washington and I was so moved by the miracle of being in this country, in this church. This man had nine children. Needless to say, we did not need to ever ask him for money. That day he took me aside and said that I was like another son to him. I was almost [physically] overwhelmed. His kindness has never left me, and to this day I always try to pay it forward."

"When we came to America, we had enough money to eventually move to the Los Angeles area since Burbank had the largest Armenian community in the U.S. Visiting relatives in Tustin, we decided to rent a house there," he continues.

Avo worked for a couple of years, then attended the University of California, Irvine, where he started with a physics major but transferred to the engineering program. He was a driven student and worked hard. He had a baccalaureate from a university in Ethiopia, and some of the units carried over to UCI, so he graduated quickly.

His first job was in El Segundo with Xerox. There, he invented a testing device and became known for this. He was recruited by Toshiba and worked with them for about ten years, using his engineering and communication skills to facilitate a connection between his Japanese corporation and U.S. companies. He had developed a finesse in working within other cultures from his multicultural experiences in Ethiopia.

Avo was then recruited by Samsung to teach them how to grow their semiconductor business. In 1995, he started dating Sherry, a Japanese woman whom he had met at Toshiba, while she was still living in Tokyo. They moved to San Jose and were married in 1997.

Today, Avo and Sherry have a daughter and a son, and the lessons in life he imparts to them starts with tolerance: do not target any community with stereotypes. He recognizes that they will never have to experience what he did in Ethiopia, much less the trauma of his parents and grandparents, but he wants them to understand the survival instinct that is still within him. That in order to "keep yourselves grounded," it is paramount they understand the importance of family and who they are.

He considers himself an American first, and, though still grounded in his religious teachings, he is not necessarily a religious person. The values of his life lessons remain strong.

"As an immigrant, I see that most immigrants are proud people. They come with the right intentions. They have a better chance of succeeding here, and finding safety. And most immigrants want to pay it forward. They know where they came from and the goodness that abounds in this country. My story is a testament to that, and I just hope we as Americans don't lose sight of this," he states.

Europeans in Egypt were generally accepted as active members of society until Gamal Abdel Nasser's presidency from 1954 to 1970. He helped to create a new Arab middle class whereby the British, Greek, French, Italian, and other foreigners have been made to feel very unwelcome and even at-risk.

On the island-nation of Cyprus, conflict between the Greek-Cypriots in the south and the Turks in the north has existed for many years. When Cyprus was part of the British Empire, a tense peace existed between these ethnic groups. Through internationally brokered agreements, Britain abdicated its control, and in 1960 the independent Republic of Cyprus was established. However, tension between the Greek-Cypriots and the Turks has remained high.

Lais

Lais was born in Cairo, Egypt, but is of Greek descent. Her father's family emigrated from Greece to Egypt, where he was born. Her mother was Greek-Cypriot but was also born in Egypt. They met through mutual friends in Cairo, later married, and had three daughters; Lais is in the middle. Her maternal grandfather was a baker who worked for the Australian army when he was stationed in the "Pacific Theater," as it was called, during World War II, and this allowed the family to be financially very comfortable. Lias's mother was a housewife, and her father worked for the water department, which was government run but provided a good income. She also remarks that her parents' love always provided a sense of safety despite what they encountered.

In 1954, when Gamal Nasser came to power in Egypt, native Arabs were emboldened to harass Europeans, and the lives of Lais's family were at risk. They had British passports because Lais's mother was Greek-Cypriot and Cyprus was still under British rule. Her father's family was originally from Greece and so, even though her father had been born in Cairo, his passport was Greek. The family was never considered Egyptian even though Lais, her siblings, and her mother had been born there. Their status was determined by their ancestry.

Lais recalls her father saying that it was no longer safe for them and that they had to leave the country quickly. He told his family that he had been in downtown Cairo during the riots: pianos and other furniture had been thrown over hotel balconies, and the rioters had screamed "Death to the Europeans!" Speaking Arabic, he, too, had screamed along with them in order to get away without being harmed.

The family convinced a doctor to write a note that Lais's mother was very sick and needed to go to Cyprus for special treatment. This ploy allowed them to flee with just the suitcases they packed, and they never returned to Egypt.

At age seven, Lais spoke French, Arabic, and Greek. She says her mom joked that Lais would even argue with their maid in Arabic. The schooling in Egypt allowed her to flourish in her early learning.

Other relatives moved from Egypt to Greece and Australia. Lais and her family took a boat to escape the trouble. It was a mass exodus of Europeans out of Egypt. They headed to Cyprus because her maternal grandmother and other relatives were there.

However, because her father had a Greek passport, he was required to go to Greece. Lais's mother would have to gather all of the necessary documents to get him back. It was supposed to take only a few weeks, but it was a year before he could rejoin his family. In the meantime, he got a job at a hotel switchboard because he spoke six languages.

"He was the sweetest man on Earth," Lais says of her father.

He told them of a time when he gave his coat to another man who was very poor and had little clothing, telling the man that he would soon be going to Cyprus so didn't need the coat. Of course, he had no idea when he would be going.

During his time in Greece, stress caused him to develop a severe ulcer. He had a small rented room and no medical care. When he eventually did get to Cyprus, no doctors wanted to treat him as they were afraid his case was too severe and he would die. However, a young surgeon who had just opened a clinic near them believed that he could, in fact, help Lais's father. The surgery was a success, which was a big relief for the family who had lost him for a year in Greece, and could have lost him to his medical condition.

He got a job in the water department in Cyprus, as he had in Egypt. This government-run department was under British rule. He loved his job and his bosses. When the British left in 1960, they wanted to move him to England, but Lais's mother did not want to leave.

When the British were in control of Cyprus, there were curfews because of rioting Greeks who wanted their independence. The Greek-Cypriot resistance fighters were known as the EOKA, and, when they were captured, many were tried and went to prison, and some were executed. Lais recalls this being a very dark time for most living in Cyprus.

In the early 1960s, even after the British had left, the island was convulsed with intercommunal skirmishes between the Turks and the Greeks. Tension between the two groups was ratcheting up, and you needed to stay in your own enclave. Lais had an aunt and uncle in Kyrenia in the north, and she recalls that once, when her family drove there to visit them, she closed her eyes tightly, fearing that at any moment they could be attacked by Turkish gangs. She imagined the horrible things that might happen to them and hoped that her parents would never to go back there. They didn't.

Later, her aunt and uncle escaped Kyrenia with nothing more than their cat.

Lais' older sister had already been married to a Greek-Cypriot, and they moved to California. From that point on her father's goal was to be "U.S. bound."

"My dad never liked Cyprus. He only stayed because my mom didn't want to leave," she says. "He was not happy at work. When the British left, his new boss was Turkish. He was a lot younger than him, and knew less. However, [the boss] would talk down to him."

She recalls an incident when one of the workers on the Turkish side of the island called her father to warn him of an ambush that was being laid for him. This likely saved his life.

Although life in Cyprus was not as bad as it had been in Egypt, her father knew that he wanted the family out of there. Lais's sister now had children in the United States, and her father wanted the rest of the family to join them.

"We left Egypt because of the turmoil. We left Cyprus under similar circumstances. When we arrived in Southern California in 1965, the riots were happening [there, too]. We wondered if we'd need to leave the U.S," she remarks.

She looks wistfully away in contemplation and then continues.

"But this is my home. This is the place that gave me and my family the opportunities to succeed. It is through my experience that makes me feel so badly for how immigrants are viewed by many people in this country."

Lais's brother-in-law sponsored the family to immigrate to America. She and her father got jobs in Southern California. His job was not necessarily at the level he'd had in previous employment, but he was grateful to be where he was.

Having been involved in the Greek Orthodox Church in Cyprus, they found an affiliation and connection with the church in Southern California. Though not particularly religious, they were observant of traditions and grateful for the merits offered by the community. This helped to ease the transition to their new world.

Today, Lais and her husband, Andrew, an immigrant from the United Kingdom, live in Northern California. They raised two children who are now adults with their own families living in Dallas and Boston.

As she reflects upon how her life changed when she and her family moved from Cyprus to the United States, she tells me of the many travels she and Andrew, and even her children, have been afforded the ability to take. In Egypt, travel was only a means of escape, and in Cyprus, there wasn't the desire to travel because maintaining a sense of stability — despite the strife that seemed to pervade the island — was of utmost importance. And with this, Lais marvels at her good fortune in coming to a place with so much opportunity and hope.

In India, the Hindu caste system is over 3,000 years old and is considered to have been developed to create order and regularity in society. There are four main categories, with Brahmins at the top; people in that caste are typically teachers and intellectuals. Out of the four main castes come 3,000 other sub-castes, plus 25,000 sub-castes that represent people's occupations.

In the rural communities, caste designations have typically been more strongly enforced than in the cities: the upper and lower castes almost always lived in segregated colonies; the water wells were not shared; upper castes would not accept food or drink from a lower caste; and one could marry only within one's caste.

Rangan

Rangan's father, Ramaswamy, was only eight years old when he ran away from his home to join a Hindu temple.

"My father knew from a very early age that he wanted to be a priest. His parents wanted their children to get a good education, but even at an early age he had his dreams set on the priesthood," Rangan says.

It was this decision by Ramaswamy that would later influence his children and wife, and it would ultimately be the catalyst to prompt his son, Rangan, to move to the United States.

His father lived in a temple, which was his home until he turned 21 and married a young girl, Vijayalakshmi, through an arranged marriage when she was only 15. This is how most marriages happened at the time in India. It still does happen this way in many of the smaller villages and towns.

The temple where his father was priest provided the family with a small home, food staples, and a religious community for them to live in. With that, however, came extreme poverty. As a priest he earned the equivalent of $2.50 a month.

"I had two sets of clothing for a whole year, and had no shoes until I was a young teenager. Poverty seemed to go hand-in-hand with devoted religious people," Rangan surmises.

His parents were both in the Brahmin caste, which is the highest to which one can belong. Castes are determined through generational lineage, but they do not produce an equivalent in economic status.

Castes in the past, and still to some extent today, stratified classes of people so that upper castes and lower castes did not co-mingle. It has been criticized for being unjust, and it often trapped people into a fixed social order that was impossible to escape. In fact, the government has changed laws over the recent decades to level the playing field for all its citizens, understanding that this rigid system causes rifts — and subsequently prejudice — between classes. However, politicians still fan the flames of classism in order to get blocks of votes from specific castes.

Rangan always questioned this system and its injustices, and ultimately he developed his own moral guideposts, ones that reflected his priest-father's notions about social justice but not about adherence to one's caste, which in his case also led to a life of poverty.

"My parents always showed us love. We were the only Brahmin in our community, and about half of the people were Muslim, but my father would teach lessons of compassion and respect for all," he says.

Tragedy struck the family in 1964 when Rangan was three years old. An older sister was in the temple playing near the lit lanterns used during a religious festival while his parents and the other siblings were outside greeting people as they left the ceremony.

Though Rangan has no recollection of it, he was told that screams emerged from inside the temple: his sister had played too close to the lanterns, and her dress caught fire. Despite efforts to douse the flames with buckets of water to save her, she died a few days later in a hospital.

Grief overwhelmed the family. Every year thereafter, when this particular festival arrived, sadness pervaded the household, and there would always be a special remembrance for her.

From a very young age, Rangan was expected to be a devoutly religious person. He learned the Vedas (holy scriptures) and could recite them, knew the *pujas* (prayers) by heart, could marry couples, wore three face-painted lines called *nama*, and had long hair pulled tightly into a bun with a small pigtail protruding from the back of his head, which was the practice of the holiest of boys and men.

Still, his father wanted his five daughters and two sons to be educated and successful. His philosophy was that one had to be strong emotionally, physically, spiritually, and socially in order to help others.

Whereas wealthy children would go to private schools, Rangan and his siblings attended public schools. He was the only Orthodox Brahmin in his class and was a target for mocking and bullying. His dad would tell him that he should be proud of who he was, not to sulk and let the others win. He advised that Rangan make friends and use humor, but fight if that was his only remaining option. Rangan chose to fight. He then allied with friends who were "tough," and his "gang" protected him. This afforded him a reputation that helped him avoid being targeted and brought a certain amount of status. It also helped that he was bright and assisted some of the lesser-inclined students to study, which resulted in their excelling in school.

The early lessons of fortitude stuck with him in that he learned not to fear anything. Later in life, when confronted with challenging problems at work, he was fair and even-keeled but would not back away.

His poverty did not get in the way of his friendships with others, even with those who had some wealth.

"We had a home, electricity, some food staples, and bamboo mats to sleep on. Nine of us lived in what was essentially two rooms. My siblings and I were not worried about being poor because we were a strong family. We were never hungry. I never felt deprived. My sisters and brother did not like it, but I did not worry about this. My father got a great deal of respect, and that was important to me."

He was known as a good student, and his ability to recite the Vedas brought admiration from others in his community.

He was a mixture of many things: religious, studious, assertive, creative, and curious, as well as a fighter for his beliefs.

His father worked at the temple seven days a week, eight hours a day. The daily ritual of lighting camphor, which he breathed in all day, would eventually cause his death. He developed severe asthma and had more and more problems breathing. Yet his devoutness persevered.

During high school, Rangan tutored local primary school children in various subjects, including English. He worked at the temple on weekends. He would later learn that many of his pupils moved on to highly professional careers. This is one of his proudest accomplishments.

Still, this was a time when he began to strongly question his caste's values. For example, his friends would come over to study, but when they ate at his house they would have to go to a separate room as it was believed that those of a lower caste could not eat with Brahmins.

"This seemed to me to be a horrible thing, and it brought about great soul-searching. How could my father preach justice and equality, but this is how we treated those not of our caste?" he says.

The money Rangan made was contributed to the household. After all, there were nine people living under one small roof. He realized that he had to provide economic stability so that he could help his family, such as paying for his siblings' education. His family, he believed then and now, is the center of his life.

Since he was a young boy, Rangan had cooked for his father while he worked at the temple. According to Hindu tradition, when the priest's wife was menstruating she could not make his meals. So, out of necessity, Rangan was called upon to do so in the temple's kitchen, which was holy and sacred, and adhered to the Vedas.

"My dad was rational in many ways. He was open about trusting me. [But] when I was in high school, he said to me 'if you eat at restaurants, or out somewhere tell me, and you will not cook for me again as you will not be purified according to our laws,'" he recalls.

As a teenager, Rangan questioned the values that he learned as a pious believer in strict Hindu rituals and traditions. It was at that time he was considering higher education. As he explored university life, he would eat at restaurants or elsewhere. He told his father as requested, and so cooking for him stopped.

There was no anger, just a realization that changes had come. When Rangan entered the University of Mysore near his home, and later went on for his master's and doctorate degrees in biochemistry, his connection to his father's strict religious tenets faded. Not that he did not feel strongly about being a Hindu, but he would never again follow the doctrine that had been laid out for him.

He also realized that, in order to be economically stable, he would need to move away from India to be further trained in clinical research. He needed to get a post-doctoral fellowship, preferably in the United States. He discussed this goal with an economics professor one day but said he would need to get a bank loan to make it a reality. Unbeknownst to him, the professor decided to loan him the 15,000 rupees to help him get under way, knowing that Rangan would repay it when he was able to do so, which he did. The compassion he received from others was certainly proportionate to the compassion he had shown to others throughout his life. The gesture the professor showed him left him speechless and humbled. It allowed him to move to the University of Texas in Tyler in 1988, and he then completed his post-doctoral work in Oakland, California, at Children's Hospital in 1991.

He had been in love with a woman he met in India while getting his master's degree at the University of Mysore, and when he went to the United States he knew that he wanted Mythreyi for his life partner. He proposed to her, she accepted, and the wedding was planned for the following year. Despite the fact that this was an inter-caste marriage between a lower caste and a Brahmin, Rangan had reconciled that it wasn't going to prevent their union — though he knew it would be seen as sacrilege to his father as well as the other temple leaders.

Rangan and Mythreyi did get married, but his father did not attend the wedding. Emotionally, this hurt Rangan deeply. He was close to his father and had always done what his dad wanted. Tension also rose for his parents, as his mother supported the marriage.

When Rangan took his new wife back to California, in protest his father stopped eating. He would have a little water and just bits of food. This was his way of showing his temple peers that he was serious about the shame his son had brought upon him.

"I was so angry," Rangan says, "that when I went back to India I needed to talk with him about my marriage. For all that I had done for him while growing up; for all the pride I had brought him at the temple; for all that he had meant to me as a father, this was how he responded. I approached my home with the intent of cutting to his very soul with my harsh words. But the moment I saw him my anger evaporated. His skeletal frame hanging like an ashen sheet took my breath away. I could not be angry with this man who had been so magnificent in my eyes. My approach quickly veered to one of contrition and compassion."

He gently said to his father, "I am wrong. This is my fault. Please do not take my error in judgment out on yourself. Do not cause pain for yourself for something that I did."

It was the custom for the father to bless the child getting married, but Rangan told his father not to bless him, even to curse him if that is what he wanted to do.

He eventually convinced his father to eat. Still, his father would barely talk to him for ten years. All of this to acknowledge to the Hindu community that his son had broken the vows of his caste, and this is how he as a priest had responded.

Prior to the wedding, he had told his son that his position as a Hindu priest required him to disavow Rangan's decision, but he also said that he would always love him.

During the ten years of limited communication with his father, Rangan would speak to him on the phone, or in person when he visited India, and update him on his work and his wife and daughter. His father would respond with little to no emotional connection. Still, Rangan didn't give up on his connection with him.

When his father became ill with severe asthma, he made amends with his son. With his time being quite limited from that point, he spoke to Rangan with the knowledge that wounds had to be healed. Conversation and professed love resumed until he died. Rangan was grateful for those remaining days that had brought a gentle ending to what had been so strained for such a long time.

Rangan often thinks about his life in the temple with his father, and on his life in pursuit of his own standing. He still practices Hinduism, and, though his wife and daughter will go to the temple for holy days, they don't share the vigor of his conviction, which he does out of respect and to connect with his father. Yet, he acknowledges that he is not in any way wedded to the doctrines of the caste he was born into, and his religious vows are in keeping with his values. His views of the world are, in many ways, based on what his father taught him: equality, hard work, justice for all, and, most especially, the importance of family.

His mother's life had been to take care of her husband and children. After her husband's death, she visited Rangan in the United States three different times. She was a big admirer of John F. Kennedy, and

Rangan took her to Washington, D.C., to Arlington National Cemetery. She stayed for six months at a time so that he could take her to visit different places in America.

Rangan sees himself as very American in so many ways, and he loves his life here. Moreover, he knows that melding his Indian culture into all that is offered here is what makes this country so unique, and it is at the core of its strength. He is, as he says, as American as you and I, with a life story that is as universal as any.

In late April 1975, after the United States had been militarily engaged in Vietnam for 17 years to combat the communists in North Vietnam, President Gerald Ford gave the order to evacuate the embassy compound in Saigon along with as many Vietnamese citizens as possible. Within 18 hours, 81 helicopters evacuated 6,000 Vietnamese and over 1,000 Americans. It was the largest helicopter evacuation in history. According to a 2015 New York Times article, an additional 130,000 people fled Saigon the day that the Viet Cong entered that city, and an estimated two million "boat people" fled Vietnam by boat and other means over the next two decades.

Wendy

Nguyet, the name given to her at birth by her parents in Saigon, was later given her American name, Wendy, when she immigrated to the United States by a sister who already lived there. She was born in 1956 into a middle-class family with two older sisters and two older brothers. Her mother, Hien, sold vegetables in an open-air market. Her father, Nghia, was a cook in the army. This was before Wendy was born. Her father left the military before her birth, and her mother stopped working in the market when Wendy was two. Her two sisters, Theresa and Mary, worked at the time, as did her brothers, Phoung and Diep. Traditionally, when children work the parents stop doing so, and they assume the role of bringing in the income and supporting their parents. In many Vietnamese families — even those in America today — this expectation often remains.

Even though the Vietnamese countryside was embroiled in war during Wendy's youth, Saigon itself was not badly affected until 1975 when the communist military rolled in. Before then, life in the city was relatively normal. "Saigon was a good place to grow up in," recalls Wendy. She and her siblings continued to live in the house that her parents owned there until she left for America.

Wendy says that, during her childhood, she was not very motivated to go to school. Still, she learned to speak Chinese and French, and she finished high school. She met her first husband when she was eighteen and had her first daughter when she was twenty.

After less than two years of marriage, her husband died in the war, two days after their daughter, Kim, was born. Of course the trauma of this took a toll on Wendy, but she had a newborn that she needed to take care of.

Both of her older sisters married Americans who were in the military. Her older sister, Mary, continued to live in Saigon when her husband moved to Iran to work, where he was gathering the documentation needed to bring his wife and child to be with him. Her mother wanted Wendy to go to Iran with Mary to help with her newborn boy, but Wendy told her mother that she had a newborn as well, and she did not want to leave Vietnam. Ultimately, Mary did not make it to Iran because the war in her own country would shape other plans.

Wendy's other sister Theresa's husband, Albert, was stationed in the Philippines, where they both still live to this day.

Albert was in Vietnam per his military assignment, and he was closely following the quickly developing events of the war as they unfolded there in spring 1975. The communists were nearing Saigon, but, to his amazement, the citizens of that city seemed not to realize the enormity of what was soon to transpire — that Saigon was about to be overrun by the communist army known as the Viet Cong, and that the Americans were going to evacuate.

At the time, Wendy was working at a newspaper company as a typesetter. One day, when she had stayed home because she wasn't feeling well, Albert brought over a document about what was transpiring in this late stage of the war, a document that was known only to U.S. military personnel, stating that an evacuation was imminent as the Viet Cong continued to push toward Saigon. Albert had his wife translate into Vietnamese the report that the country's collapse was very near and that they should leave immediately. Wendy's family was in disbelief; her parents and brothers, especially, were in denial. Saigon would not fall to the communists, they thought; the government in Saigon had said that there was now peace in the countryside, which is why the Americans were going to leave. However, Wendy was unsure about the government's pronouncements because she had heard some radio broadcasts from the rural areas of Vietnam that said war was still going on. She was confused and did not necessarily believe what Theresa had said, either. Still, she wanted to find some solace somewhere after her husband was killed, and going to the Philippines for respite sounded like a good idea in any event. Within a few days, Wendy, her sister Mary, and their children left Vietnam.

As their boat entered the port in Manila, they were told by the Philippine government that they could not land there, so their ship was sent to Guam. It was in Guam that they were informed that Vietnam had collapsed and that the communists had indeed taken over Saigon, along with the rest of the country. It was also at that time that the Americans were evacuating Vietnam.

With little else than a small suitcase, Wendy, Mary, and their children were now without a country. Still, there was a boat ready to take Vietnamese back to their country. Little did they know that this boat was actually taking people back to the horror of what was taking place back home and, for most, imprisonment. Albert sternly told them not to leave.

Meanwhile, her brothers and parents had stayed back in Vietnam. They survived, though Wendy wouldn't know how difficult it was for them until 13 years later when they were finally able to contact one another.

She remained in Guam for only two days in a refugee camp. Though her stay in the camp was not harsh, she now knew that she could not go home. Overwhelming grief took over with the realization that she no longer even had a home.

Albert bought plane tickets to take Wendy and her sister and children to Camp Pendleton in the United States, where refugees were first taken. His mother lived near San Bernadino, California, and she invited Wendy, Mary, and their children to stay with her. Albert also did the legwork to get the family green cards and social security numbers. He was clearly instrumental in getting them to safety and ensuring that their transition to new lives in America would begin.

Wendy speaks of the distress and anxiety she felt, not being able to talk to or even write letters to her parents. The communists in Vietnam were very restrictive about any communication with people who lived abroad, especially in the United States. She describes her feelings as being an overwhelming homesickness that stayed with her for the years she did not have contact with her family. Meanwhile, her parents had no idea where she was.

Wendy worked sewing tennis nets for a company in Long Beach for two months. She then went to bartending school and worked for a short time in a Japanese restaurant tending bar. She landed a long-term bartending job in her sister Mary's newly purchased karaoke bar. In 1985, she married a man who was also from Vietnam, and they had two more children, Brian and Amy. They lived in Long Beach, California, where Wendy had worked as a card dealer in a local casino. Her marriage was troubled, and it led to divorce seven years later, but her determination to fend for her family only strengthened. In 1993 she took her children to Oakland.

In 1988, Wendy's sister Mary had written a letter and sent it, along with money sewn into the leg of a pair of pants, in the hope that the package would get to their parents. There was no certainty that it would reach its destination; the communist government would not allow letters and packages from the United States to come to Vietnam. So Mary sent it from Los Angeles to Paris, where she had a friend, who then rerouted it to Vietnam. Happily, they got a response from a relative three months later that their parents had indeed received the package. Their parents and brothers now learned that Wendy, Mary, and the children were safe.

After that, in 1990, Mary became the first family member to go back to Vietnam. In 1991, Wendy also returned to see her parents and brothers for the first time in 16 years.

Her return was incredibly emotional. She didn't tell her parents that she was coming back as she wanted it to be a surprise. She took her young son, Brian, with her. With tears streaming down her cheeks, she knocked on a familiar door, and her stunned parents welcomed her with tears of their own.

Wendy and her children have been to Vietnam many times since 1991. Her parents are both deceased, but her brothers and their families, as well as other relatives, remain in Saigon. Life in Vietnam has changed drastically over the past few decades. Tourism is now a key industry, and governmental restrictions have relaxed significantly.

For Wendy, the shock of having to leave her home country, not knowing what the future held, only subsided when she lived in Long Beach in 1985. It took those ten years to feel comfortable with her new life in America. Even with the tumultuous departure from

Vietnam, not knowing of her family's status in her home country, and the challenge of finding her place in the United States, she feels that America has offered her and her children the best opportunities they could have.

"This is my home," she says proudly.

According to the U.N.'s Global Database on Violence against Women (2017), Guatemala has one of the highest rates of violence against women and girls in the world. Although government reforms have attempted to address this, the situation is still often dire. Femicide (the systemic murder of women and girls), for example, ranks third behind El Salvador and Jamaica. The civil war between the government and the indigenous rebel groups who were fighting a history of discrimination, and even attempted genocide, ended after 36 years in 1991 after a peace accord was reached. However, poverty and limited economic reforms remain to this day. Many of those who emigrate from Guatemala seek the safety and economic security not offered to all in the country today.

Mimi

Mimi was born in a small town called La Tinta Alta Verapaz in Guatemala in 1969. Located in the Polochic River Valley, this hot and humid region consists mostly of small family-owned farms that produce little income, primarily growing crops for their own use. Mimi was one of seven children with loving parents, though her mother could be somewhat exacting. All but one of her older siblings went to college, and, given school costs, there was often not enough money for food. Yet education for the children was critical to her parents; they understood that this would give their children greater access to future opportunities. It was not common in their town for teens to go to college, and, though it may have been her parents' desire, Mimi did not want to go down that path.

La Tinta was named after the Jiquilite leaf, which, when crushed by stone, bleeds an indigo dye. Begun by German colonists in the late 1800s, making the dye became part of the local industry. The inhabitants at that time would create large cement pits to squeeze the leaves and collect the ink.

Like the Jiquilite leaf, Mimi's life at the age of 16 was slowly but inexorably being drained of its vibrancy.

Daniela, Mimi's daughter, who translates her mother's native Spanish into English, describes her mother's upbringing. Mimi's father worked for a government program called "Malaria," for which he would go to villages around the country for three months at a time to assist the locals in preventing the spread of the disease.

When he was a soldier, before his government job, he met Mimi's mother while in one of these towns when she was 15. Later, while traveling together for his job, they came upon La Tinta and decided to make it their home. They bought some land to farm, settled in, and grew crops for their own sustenance as well as to sell to supplement her father's government salary.

"Even though my grandmother was the person to work the land, and it was essentially hers, because of how women were viewed my grandfather was on the title and not her," notes Daniela.

The land was 30 minutes from her house, so when Mimi's mother didn't walk there to tend to the coffee beans, rice, and other crops, she had some tenants who lived on the farm to take care of the crops. However, she later discovered that these workers were taking some of the produce and selling it for themselves.

Mimi only went to school until sixth grade. Despite most of her siblings going to college, Mimi never had an interest in getting an education. Since going to school was not compulsory, she didn't go.

She met Ceferino at age 16 and became pregnant. Being afraid of her parents' reaction, she ran away. She married Ceferino two years later, after she had Daniela and a one-year-old son.

Her husband lived in La Democracia, Huehuetenango, a small city in Guatemala near the northwest border with Mexico. It, too, is a mainly agricultural region, although Ceferino was not interested in farming. At first he was a mail carrier, but he couldn't keep any job long enough to sustain any form of reasonable lifestyle for his wife and children.

"I lived at my husband's house with my in-laws. My father-in-law was very kind to me, but my mother-in-law was not," she recalls.

Mimi's husband was violent.

"Ceferino would come home drunk and order me around. If I did not obey him fast enough, he would hit me. His mother would encourage him to hurt me — for disrespecting her son, she would say," Mimi tearfully recalls.

Her father-in-law would do what he could to keep her safe. He, too, was living within the confines of a household rife with abuse. He was alive for four years while Mimi was there and did what he could to protect her, even to the point of having her sleep in the spare bed in his bedroom, which was separate from his wife. After his death, Mimi no longer had her father-in-law's protection. She was not "allowed" to leave the home, and she essentially cleaned and cooked for her husband and his mother. There was no TV or radio and little distraction outside of her chores. She felt enslaved.

As happens in most domestic violence households, Ceferino isolated Mimi from the outside world.

Their claims of being a devout Christian family belied their treatment of Mimi.

"One day in the late stages of my pregnancy with my first child, I visited my parents, and while there danced with a brother-in-law at a family party. When I returned, and having given birth to my daughter only ten days before, my husband learned that I had danced back in La Tinta. I was making salsa with hot peppers, onions, and other spices to add to the tomatoes. In a rage, he smeared the salsa in my eyes. His mother did nothing. In fact, she egged him on, saying that I was a whore and deserved it."

The torture was unrelenting.

Choking back tears, Mimi recalls the harshness of her existence in that home.

"I left my parents' home because I was pregnant, and afraid. I couldn't return there because I would have shamed my family. But now, I was living a life of hell," she says.

Mimi chose not to tell her family where she was living, but her mother found out where, and she stayed with Mimi for a couple of weeks until her son was born. She had an idea of what was happening but was shielded from the extent of the trauma her daughter was experiencing. Mimi wanted to leave, but her confusion anchored her waist-deep in indecision.

At this point, with a quiet defiance and intensity of conviction rising within her, Daniela weighs in on the desperation her mother tearfully describes.

"I don't have hate for my father, but I don't want him around. I don't want him as a grandfather to my kids. I want nothing to do with him."

As I listen to Daniela, I wonder how she could *not* hate him. The abuse was pervasive. Daniela and her brother and sister don't recall much of the trauma, having blocked it from their consciousness with a self-protective veil.

Daniela is a sweet, loving mother to her own two young children. She is caring and protective of her mother, as well. Forgiveness seems to be in her heart. There is a gentleness that she shares with her mother, her husband, and those around her.

Mimi lived in her husband and his mother's home until her children were ages 5, 4, and 3. Suddenly, and without discussion, Ceferino decided to move to Chiapas, Mexico.

While Mimi had been away, visiting her family in La Tinta, Mimi's father-in-law had given his son a house with land on a coffee plantation. The coffee beans were ready to be picked and sold, but Ceferino inexplicably sold it to a step-brother. He then used that money from the sale of the house and land on alcohol and other vices, so it was never used to support his family. Virtually penniless, he decided to move them to Chiapas where he had relatives. Saying nothing to Mimi about where they were going to live or how they would support themselves, he brought his wife and children into a life of great poverty. Mimi's heart sank lower, but what could she do?

They moved into abandoned horse stables. No walls, dirt floors, no doors, no electricity, and no running water. Mimi made a fire pit to boil water and to cook. They lived there for three years, surviving in almost surreal conditions.

"We were isolated from most people. My husband would go into town to drink and carouse. He didn't work, and continued to treat me horribly. For three years my children had no shoes and very little clothing. Except for the little one, they would walk to school on dirt roads a long way," she recalls.

Her husband spent whatever money he had. His relatives in Chiapas gave him some land, and he grew some vegetables to feed the family. A few tomatoes, a little corn, but that was about it.

"We were hungry. Many times I had to find a wild plant to make soup," Mimi says.

One day in 1991, she'd had enough. She escaped with her children, moving back to La Tinta with her mother and father. That same year, Ceferino moved north to the United States.

After a month of being with her mom, who felt it was her duty to tell Mimi how to mother her children, things changed again.

First, they moved back to Ceferino's mother's house. Mimi would rather have had her mother-in-law, who treated her children well, give her a hard time than her own mother, who didn't treat the children very kindly. During the two years she lived there, her husband tried to convince her that he had changed. He eventually sent money to help get her to the United

States, and he made arrangements to have her taken there.

She didn't want to leave her children. She was frightened and skeptical.

Her husband's sister confronted Mimi, and her low self-esteem kicked in. She felt that she had to go even if it meant leaving her children behind with his mother. She vowed that she would make enough money to send for them someday.

The journey past the border was harrowing for her. She was taken through the desert to cross, but was caught and returned to Mexico. She tells of the conditions to cross: the heat, the thirst, the hunger. Still, she desperately wanted to be in a position to get her children to a better life. The second attempt was successful.

Being with her husband again was traumatic, however. Those four years in the San Francisco Bay Area were a continuation of isolation and abuse. He, of course, had not changed. Mimi was depressed, but she knew that Ceferino held the power of applying (or not) for residency for Mimi and her children, so she needed to be cautious.

The only time the children could speak to Mimi by phone was for them to take a five-hour drive to a place where there was access to a telephone.

From what Daniela recalls, she was more worried about her mother than she was for herself and her siblings.

"We were being taken care of. We had food and a place to sleep. We had moved back in with my mother's mother. But my mother was with [Ceferino] in a strange place, knowing no one."

After two years, Mimi and her husband had gotten visas for their children to travel to the United States, but the kids didn't want to go. They were understandably anxious about moving to the unknown. It would take another two years before they could be convinced to emigrate.

Daniela and her siblings were right to be worried.

At one point, in a drunken rage, Ceferino had beaten Mimi, choked her, and threatened that, if she called the police, he would stop the paperwork to bring her children to the states.

Her courage was beginning to build, however. She recalls fantasizing about killing him, but to do so would have put her in jail, and she'd never see her children again. Still, she got him to move out of their apartment, and she was determined to fend for herself.

In 1997, Daniela and her siblings arrived. Mimi had a one-room apartment where she, the children, and her sister lived. Ceferino would float in and out of their lives, sometimes staying with them and sometimes not. Sometimes he had a construction job, and sometimes not. His instability lingered, but Mimi was now much more in control of her life.

She had two jobs: one was cleaning an office building, and the other was packaging food in the evenings at a small food processing plant. While she was at work, her sister took care of the children.

Mimi now had a little income to support herself and her children. If Ceferino was staying with them and got drunk, she would send him away. She was torn at times, because she wanted him to be a real father to their children and hoped that he had changed. But, of course, he did not.

One day in 1998, he came storming into their apartment announcing that he was going to send the children back to Guatemala if she did not take him back.

"He came up the stairs in a frightening way, yelling that he would send them back," she recalls.

"I took out a knife and told him that, if he dared to come up to take them away, he'd have to get past me first."

She pushed him down the stairs, and he tumbled helplessly to the bottom. She had liberated herself from what seemed like a lifetime of torture in that one moment of triumph.

They only saw him sporadically after that.

Mimi and her children moved to another apartment in another part of the Bay Area. Since then, her children have had their struggles. Her son is trying to combat the demons that clearly have been the result of his early life trauma. Her youngest daughter has had to summon her strength to battle her own woes but is managing as best she can.

Daniela exudes a resilience and strength that marks a quiet fierceness that will not allow her upbringing to deter her.

As for Mimi, she lives in an apartment with a partner who treats her with respect. She is not married, and may not ever be again. Still, she is at peace. She and Daniela have their own housecleaning business, and they are doing just fine.

"I went through hell for many years, but I have gone past that. We are settled into our lives here in America, living comfortably and with self-respect. As horrible as things had been from the age of 16, I have no regrets because the one good thing Ceferino gave me was my children," she says.

With that, Mimi smiles at the good fortune she now has in America.

Los Zetas, the drug cartel that has been responsible for thousands of murders in Mexico, has gripped the public with fear and with distrust, because citizens see that the cartels have influenced the government and police with bribery, and thus little is being done about the violence. In witness testimony in Texas courts recently, accounts describe Mexican politicians receiving money for their electoral campaigns and police being paid to look the other way as hundreds of people are massacred or disappear in one state alone, Coahuila. And this scenario is happening all over Mexico.

Alvaro

It was Alvaro's father who taught him that change requires adaptation, and adaptation determines survival.

Raised in Monterrey in the state of Nuevo Leon, Mexico, in the 1960s, Alvaro spent a lot of time with family and friends in Tampico, in the state of Tamaulipas. His passion for business was driven by his father, sold shoes and often brought his son along with him. Alvaro learned a great deal in those days, especially about having to adapt. When Chinese shoe manufacturers took over that line of business in Monterrey, his father went into real estate and other business ventures, which kept the family living comfortably. As a business major at a university in Monterrey, Alvaro knew that this was in his blood.

Dabbling in some business ventures resulted in him quitting school, and he started his own businesses selling cars as well as shoes. With the realization that he needed to return to his studies, and at the prodding of his father, he went back to school to finish his degree and, following graduation, worked for a couple of different companies.

In 2000, Alvaro started his own company selling light construction equipment to building contractors. Working seven days a week, he grew the business. His hard work, however, likely led to Los Zetas and other crime families seeing opportunity in his success.

What happened in the subsequent 12 years shaped a decision he had no choice but to make. When confronted with his sister's encounter with the threats from a ruthless drug cartel, he knew he and his family had to leave Mexico.

"Although I didn't fear them for myself, it was my family that was at risk of being kidnapped and killed," he says.

In the early 2000s, Alvaro tried to protect his wife, Rosario, from what was happening in his world.

He typically would not tell her of the dangers that were lurking, but she knew that crime in their city was beginning to escalate.

Los Zetas is among the most merciless drug cartels in all of Mexico. Extortion is one of the ways it has gained enormous wealth. Disappearances of those who don't abide by the cartel's terms are commonplace. Dismembering its victims, sending body parts to families that in any way crossed it, and showing no regard for any protestation on the part of those perceived to have slighted it, is the norm. For Alvaro, he, his family, and his friends were now entangled in the brutal web that gripped not just their region but all of Mexico.

"In 2006, a friend of mine was kidnapped, and 11 days after that he had to pay one million pesos. He moved away for a month with no communication to anyone to ensure that friends and family would be safe," Alvaro says.

Upon the friend's return, he told Alvaro that he and his family were going into hiding for their safety.

"They called me [too]," Alvaro tells me he said to his friend, "and threatened me while I was in my office at work."

The caller said that men were waiting outside the building with guns ready to shoot Alvaro if he didn't pay them what they wanted.

"I was frightened and pissed off, but I didn't know how real this threat is."

"I feel I *had* to pay," said his friend, "but what will you do?"

"Right now I will take my chances. I don't want them to think that they can push me around," Alvaro replied.

With trepidation, he had cautiously emerged from his shop, but no guns appeared. This threat was not real. Yet this was a harbinger of things to come. He wondered if the friend who had been kidnapped had given up his name under duress. He went to the friend and asked if his name had been given to the tormentors — if so, Alvaro recalls, he would pack up his suitcase and take his family into hiding immediately. The friend would only meet him in a parking lot at a convenience store because he was being harassed again, as well. He put Alvaro's mind at ease, earnestly assuring him that he didn't give Alvaro's name to the kidnappers.

Reflecting on how he had attracted the attention of this threat, Alvaro wonders aloud whether the ads he put in the Yellow Pages led them to his business.

Extortion in Monterrey was growing. In addition to Los Zetas, other gangs had begun to emulate their ways.

"I didn't know who had called me. I wondered if I was dealing with the Zetas, and I knew that these guys were not to be messed with. I don't believe it was them, but others tried to use their methods, so I had my suspicions."

This was not the first time Alvaro had been confronted with crime. As a way to generate business in the early days, he would drive to construction sites out in the desert to see if he could sell equipment to the builders. Housing was burgeoning in the deserts. There was an expansion of communities into areas that were untapped. Moving away from the city was becoming more desirable.

Returning from a visit to a housing construction site in the desert after dark, as the dust and tumbleweeds blew past his car, Alvaro describes how shadowy figures leapt out in front of the vehicle to get him to stop, likely so they could rob him. He almost ran over them but, realizing immediately what was transpiring, he sped up and didn't stop until he reached his home, anxiously checking the rearview mirror to assure himself that he was not being followed.

Los Zetas was known to bury bodies and body parts out in the desert. As Alvaro had learned, robbers were becoming a fixture there, too. He realized that this approach to getting new customers was too dangerous, so he stopped driving to the desert.

However, even traveling freeways posed a problem, as those roads were getting dangerous, too. What you imagined was a routine traffic stop by the police could actually be a shake-down. You could be robbed, or worse; your name and description could be given to the cartel if you didn't cooperate. Trust was becoming a precious commodity.

"You couldn't rely on the police as they were on the take. They were surely not to be trusted. It was known that the information you gave up to them could easily end up in the wrong hands," he says.

The middle and upper-middle classes were now the most vulnerable because the rich had either left Mexico or had body guards.

"When my son, Alvarito, who is now 25, was 12, the situation started getting bad. Still, I tried to protect my sons, even my second son, Leo, who is six years younger than Alvarito; [they] needed to stay closer to home," he says.

Alvarito knows now that his father would keep his anxiety to himself to protect his family from the worry that would surely ensue.

"Although my mother knew what was going on in the city, she may not have realized how this was affecting my father," Alvarito notes. Looking back now, he sees that his father was protecting him and his brother, too, by not giving them too much information about what he was confronting on a regular basis.

Alvaro needed to be smart, strong, and even stoic in order to protect his family. Yet the tension of life in the crosshairs of the gangs was clearly affecting him. How to survive, and especially how to protect his family, took front and center in his life.

Among friends, family, and neighbors, an informal network of communication was set up using Twitter. Many people in the neighborhood would relay via social media where trouble was at any given moment.

"You knew what streets and neighborhoods to avoid, learning that gunshots were just heard, or that a kidnapping had just taken place. This was one way we devised to protect ourselves," he recalls.

"I don't think my sons understood the dangers during that time. The cartel would take kids and use them as human shields if they got into gunfights with rivals, or they would extort these kids' families."

Thinking back to what he had learned from his own father when he was younger, Alvaro says, "When you are confronted with this, you just have to adjust your lives and expectations. This was our new way of trying to live a normal life."

He continues, "Alvarito was going to parties as a young teen, like anyone of his age. The families of the homes that hosted the parties would have party-goers stay over until daylight, when it was safer to leave."

The homes were like those in any suburb anywhere. Manicured lawns, leafy trees, garages, and yards. Yet the outward appearance of the pastoral neighborhood was cloven between safe passage and dangerous pathways.

One day Leo called his dad. He was 12 at the time, and was at a mall.

Alvaro tells what happened but chokes up, clearly emotional to this day at the thought of his young son being threatened.

"Dad, he said, "these guys threatened to hurt me if I didn't give them my cell phone," fear emanating over the phone.

"You are at the mall, so head to the first restaurant nearby, and I will get you," Alvaro responded.

He asked his older son to join him as they jumped into the car and raced to find Leo.

"We will find him, and then I will go after the punks who threatened him. I can't deal with this anymore," he says he told Alvarito, with fear and anger rising in his voice.

"It was the longest ride I've ever taken."

He found Leo, who was unhurt but shaken, but could not find the little gang.

Leo described those who threatened him as roughly 16- and 17-year-olds. The group probably formed as a result of the lawlessness that had taken hold of the city. Alvaro was beginning to think about what was needed to leave the daily horror that his family and friends were being subjected to.

Trust in those you didn't know, whom you thought would be honest, like the police, could no longer be counted on. Only the military, which was at times deployed to quell desperate situations of gang-related drug activity, was considered reliable by the citizens. But this intervention wasn't widespread, and both the real cartels and those who mimicked them continued to flourish.

"Anyone could get a gun and say they were Zeta. They could be, you would never know," Alvaro says.

"Los Zetas were kidnapping young kids and pulling them inside a van or car. They would take them, and they would force them to be dependent on drugs, so they would work for them. The boys would deliver drugs, or be used as human shields in shootouts. The girls were their sex slaves. Early on parents called the police, but the police would give their names up to the Zetas," he recalls.

By the time Alvarito was going to college in San Francisco, California, in 2011, Leo was not allowed to go to a park to play or to the mall without his father's presence. It had become far too dangerous.

After Alvaro and his wife, Rosario had gotten married, and before the widespread violence had erupted, they got an apartment in a complex that was considered safe at the time. However, his mom owned an apartment in a crime-ridden neighborhood that his sister, Yola, insisted on living in so she could feel a sense of independence. The final straw was about to unfold.

Yola phoned one day quite upset. After going out to her car in the driveway, she noticed that papers were strewn about inside the car and that compact discs were out of place. She looked carefully around the interior for other things that were out of place, and she went to the back of the car to open the trunk to see if other things had been moved. To her shock, a man jumped out and dashed through the open gate. She called the police and her brother.

The police came, and they found the intruder nearby. Something strange was happening, however. Across the street from the apartment, a car with dark-tinted windows was parked nearby, with one window slightly open. The ominous presence of the vehicle was felt by Alvaro and Yola. The police joined them upstairs in Yola's apartment to provide information about the incident. When they came back outside, the mysterious car had disappeared, but the eerie coincidence of the man in the trunk, the police arriving to find the intruder, and that strange car raised the concerns and suspicions of the two siblings.

In addition, the police did not accurately report what Yola stated to them. Alvaro confronted the two cops and said that he would "beat the hell" out of them if they did not change their report. He was that angry.

"At that point I was fed up with what had been taking place in my city," he says. The next day in the news the crime was reported, but, due to "insufficient evidence," the intruder was released from jail.

"We did what we were supposed to in reporting the crime. There's nothing more we could have done," Alvaro says. The corruption, the fear, and the insanity of it all marked a turning point in his resolve to save his family.

"I took bedsheets, and asked Yola what she would normally wear, and what other items were important for her daily life."

She told him. He put clothing and the other accessories into the sheets, knotted them to secure a homemade duffle bag, and took her to their parents' place in a safer part of town despite her protestations.

The pressure would only continue to build, however.

His pick-up truck had some recognizable stickers and marks. One needed to be aware that anything could be identified as connected to that person's identity.

"Alvarito took my truck without letting me know, because he was in a choreography group and had a *quinceanera* to dance at," he says.

Alvaro was very upset because criminals could recognize that the truck was his, and his son could be at risk.

"You see," he says, "Yola worked as a secretary for a very wealthy businessman. She would be an easy target for extortion. She could easily be tortured and killed. When they saw my truck in front of her apartment that day, I could be targeted, as well."

Alvaro alerted his father to what Alvarito had done. Despite his father at first not recognizing the danger that his grandson was in, he soon got the point, and they drove to get Alvarito out of fear for his safety.

That was truly the last straw. Alvaro knew that he had to arrange for his family to leave the country. His business went bust because he could no longer go to his office very frequently as it was not safe. He was trying to keep it running from afar, but the employees now seemed to be driving it into ruins.

"I can't do this anymore, Rosario," he told his wife. "I am trying to be strong for all of us, but it is overwhelming, and we have to protect our boys."

He had learned of an online program to become certified as a teacher in Canada, Australia, or the U.S. in Texas, where bilingual education was being taught. He studied every night, and within eight months got the certificate. He moved to Dallas with his family, including his parents. Yola would join them later. That was in 2012.

Today, Alvaro, Rosario, and Leo have permanent status because he has been employed in a local school district in the Dallas area for over five years now. Alvarito, who came to the United States on a student visa to go to San Francisco State University, is the only one that has had to apply for multiple temporary visas because he didn't emigrate with his parents under his father's status. Upon graduation, Alvarito worked as a programmer in Silicon Valley and is currently attending graduate school on the East Coast. Despite living over eight years legally in the United States, he still has no permanent status, and may have to return to Mexico after his studies.

Alvaro still has strong business acumen, and he has a few ideas that he would like to pursue if he can get funding.

The danger he and his family were subjected to in Monterrey shaped their future. Despite all of his resolve to live there, the cataclysmic nature of crime in Mexico forced his hand.

"Still, I have experienced anti-Latino sentiment here, and it bothers me. I am not here to take someone's job, or commit crime. I am here because I needed to make life safe for my family," he says.

He acknowledges that the lifestyle they had in Mexico because of his business was far more secure financially than they are in Dallas, but safety is his primary concern. Still, he laments the fact that he was forced to leave his home. He puts it to me this way: "When I was in Mexico, I didn't have to think twice if I needed four new tires for my truck. Here, I have to delay or not purchase something [else] we want in order to get those tires."

The trade-off was literally a matter of life and death, however. He can breathe easier knowing that they have adapted to Dallas, a place that requires much less in the way of ensuring safety for him and his family, and in a country that affords his children the opportunity to reach their potential. And yet, he admits, "I am not sure what I consider home, or where we will be truly welcomed."

Italy, like so many European countries, has its origins in ancient history well before there were delineated political borders. Its culture has been shared throughout the world in the form of science, food, art, clothing, language, and religion. It has also known very dark times. Waves of Italian immigrants found their way to the United States at the end of the nineteenth and into the middle of the twentieth centuries. More recently, Fascism and Nazi occupation during World War II caused many Italians to seek the opportunities that America promised to those who came.

(For this interview, I should clarify at the outset that Pina is my wife. Her story, and the current status of immigration policy in America, inspired me to write this book. —JS)

Pina

Pina's family emigrated from Italy with no less hope and determination than my own Jewish ancestors from Eastern Europe. They wanted to live in a place that accepted others regardless of circumstances, and that offered opportunities not accessible in their countries of origin.

There were so many times when I entered Pina's house in Utica, New York, that I felt a warmth, a closeness that her family embodied. The smell of tomato sauce simmering on the stove in the small kitchen, with its ladles and wooden stirring spoons hanging above. Pina's mother, Margherita (or Mamma, as she was called by everyone, even non-relatives), absentmindedly moving the spoon around the rich, aromatic liquid, readying it for a sumptuous meal of pasta, followed by *i secondi* of meatballs, sausage, greens fried in garlic and olive oil, and fresh Italian bread.

My Jewish upbringing, with its limited fare mostly due to my mother's less than enthusiastic menu, though cooked with no less love, had not introduced me to such bounty. Italian food to me — before I met Pina — consisted of Pic-a-Pizza, a local joint with decent pies smothered in cheese and thick circles of greasy pepperoni. It was also, according to my mom's culinary acumen, Waldbaum's Supermarket-brand spaghetti, jarred tomato sauce, with ground beef added to enhance the orange broth, melded together in a well-worn aluminum pot and served from said pot mid-table with the three Sher boys hungrily lapping up the home-brewed suburban cuisine.

Pina's house was a three-story wooden structure where she and her family lived on the main floor, and renters, when there were any, lived on the second and third floors. On a street named Webster Avenue, bordered by a cemetery just down the block and Eannace Funeral Home within view of the backyard, the house tilted slightly, earning the nickname I assigned to it, "The Leaning Tower of Web."

And yet the warmth that exuded from the house because of its inhabitants fascinated me. Growing up in a lower-middle-income neighborhood on Long Island, I never wanted for anything, yet I knew that my teacher-father and office-worker-mother would never garner the types of incomes that some of my fellow students' families had.

Pina's house was also in a lower-income neighborhood, but the contrast to mine was stark. Although I, too, had a strong family presence within miles of my home, she was from an Italian family the likes of which I had not known. Since her parents didn't speak English, Italian was the language of choice. Moreover, in the neighborhood church, grocery store, butcher, pastry shop, and hardware store, most of the patrons spoke in that same tongue. I took two courses in Italian in college, jokingly claiming that I took them for "defensive purposes" to know what her parents were saying about me! Although certainly not bi-lingual, I knew enough to know that they seemed to like me.

My family had a strong Jewish religious and cultural connection, so in some ways we and Pina's family were quite similar. The immigrant roots were different, the reasons for emigration different, yet the promise of new opportunity and freedom to pursue dreams unencumbered were the same.

As she gazes intently into her past, my wife of 37 years thinks about the question I had just posed about her life in Italy. Through her dark, almost somber eyes, her mind travels to the day her father, Dante, left the family from the tiny village of San Donato Val di Comino in 1959 to join his daughter Mirella and her husband, Dominick, in Utica.

Dominick, a U.S. army private stationed in Germany in 1954 and 1955, had journeyed to Italy to accompany an army buddy who wanted to visit a relative in Settefrati, a town near San Donato. As it happened, that same day Mirella had walked the four miles to Settefrati to help her grandfather with an errand. Dominick was smitten by the then-16-year-old Mirella, who, the following year (the year that Pina was born), married Dominick and made what was a dizzying journey with a man she barely knew, to a place undeniably different from anything she had ever known. After over 63 years of marriage, they remain the driving force behind what was to come for Pina and her family.

When her father left to join Dominick's business in the United States, Pina can only recall the trauma.

"My parents, six of my siblings, and other various relatives piled into the small uncomfortable cars as we headed to the port in Naples to see him off."

The undeniable truth was that the poverty surrounding them, despite the efforts of the people in San Donato and surrounding towns to survive in a barter system economy, had won out.

At four years old, Pina was simply too young to grasp that her father was one of many immigrants that had sought, over two centuries, the opportunity that was promised in the United States. With no job other than being a bricklayer for a pittance in Italy, he had the chance to make some "real money" by doing masonry work for Dominick's construction company.

Still, the feeling of devastation of being apart from their father and husband overwhelmed the household. It would not be until 1962 that most of the family would reunite in Utica.

Pina recalls that, "In San Donato we were very poor. I shared a bed in our small house with two of my sisters. We had to fetch water for cooking and cleaning, and wood for warmth. My mother, who was an amazing woman, always made sure we had food on the table."

Winters were cold and could be snowy. The mountain winds prevailed upon the houses with a rush of dread; survival was the predominant preoccupation for the hardened townspeople.

"My mother was strong. She was a mail carrier for the town, delivering letters [to the houses] along the stone streets. She carried wood on her head for burning in our stove for heat, and water in a basin, also balanced instinctively on her head. She held us together. She was also in a continual state of almost hyper-humility to a point that affected me and some of my siblings' self-esteem," says Pina.

What had befallen San Donato during World War II likely contributed to that anxiety and fear, which carried over to future generations.

Today, San Donato is a beautiful town built up onto the rugged Apennine Mountains between Naples and Rome. The houses are constructed with calcareous stone carved from the nearby mountains, with walls thick enough to keep out the summer heat as well as insulate from the winter cold. The arched, thick wooden doors lead to the stone enclaves awaiting inside. Many of the trees that dot the countryside are olive, lending to its uniquely Italian appearance. The town's main square, or *piazza*, is the central forum for most activities, including the bar, a couple of restaurants, *la panetteria* (the bakery), *il macellaio* (the butcher), and the post office. It retains a medieval charm that is known to those who explore Italian hill towns. It is a close-knit place where you can walk no more than a few feet before running into a cousin, an aunt, or a villager who knows your cousin and aunt.

According to scholars, the history of San Donato dates back to the ancient Romans and then to the Lombards.

"It was formed as a town in the eighth century around the small church of San Donato that was itself formed around a fortress like many medieval towns. Despite devastating earthquakes, it would survive the many centuries of change to retain its beauty and fervent Catholic beliefs" (from LifeinItaly.com).

In the 1940s, the Nazis occupied the town. San Donato offered a vantage point to control the lower valley and the route from Lazio to Abruzzi — two Italian regions. Much of the damage to the town was aerial bombardment by the Americans and the British Air Force.

Margherita rarely spoke of the war or of how it affected her and her family. Little is known by the younger family members, either because they were not alive at the time or they were not privy to the inner turmoil that must have plagued their mother, their older siblings, and all of San Donato. Dante was in the Italian army stationed in Ethiopia for some of that time.

According to the article "The Holocaust Story from the White Pages" by Michael Frank in *Tablet* magazine (July 2017), the passage of racial laws under Benito Mussolini in 1938 meant that "foreign Jews" — those from countries other than Italy — were to be "interned" in small towns or sent to one of the 48 prisoner-of-war camps established throughout the country. Of the 4,000 Jews remaining in Italy after it entered the war in 1940, 44 were sent to San Donato.

In the towns, Jews lived under *confine libero*, or house arrest. They lived off of a very small per diem, sold possessions, or did odd jobs. Each family had to check in frequently with local authorities, and none knew what would happen to them.

Food was scarce for everyone, but, for the interned Jews, reliance on local people to feed and clothe them was the only means of survival. Margherita was one of those who saw the desperation felt by those in confinement in their town, and she risked her own safety to ensure that these people survived.

Since the Nazis would eventually occupy the town, many of the Jews went into hiding in the nearby foothills.

One of Pina's older siblings, Anna, told her that their brother Fernando would take food and clothing up to the cave where a Jewish family, the Levis, were in hiding. If he were to run into German soldiers, he would explain that he was looking for wood, or searching for wild mushrooms.

In 1944, only months before the Allies would liberate Italy, the Nazis made one last push to deport Jews from their internment to their deaths in Auschwitz. Many of San Donato's Jews understood that they had to flee into the surrounding hills. Still, the Nazis flushed out some of them by offering food and clothing, knowing that the Jews were desperate. Those who were discovered in San Donato, or those who came down from the hills, were rounded up and sent to their deaths in the concentration camp. Only four of them survived the ordeal.

An overwhelming feeling of loss and grief gripped the townspeople as those Jews who had been part of their lives were sent to their deaths. This would shape what was to come for Pina's family and all the residents of San Donato.

Following the war, Dante, Fernando, and Dante's brother, Remo, found work cutting stone and laying it to rebuild Monte Cassino, which had been one of the most influential monasteries in Europe dating back to the mid-sixth century. It was the site where Benedict, who was later canonized as a saint, and the Benedictine monks established the role of monasticism in the Catholic Church.

The Battle of Monte Cassino in 1944, which was seen by the Allies as critical to taking Rome, had cost the lives of more than 55,000 Allied soldiers and 22,000 Germans. For Dante, Fernando, and Remo, the exhausting work to help rebuild the monastery would take ten years; they traveled 38 kilometers by bus from San Donato every Monday morning and returned every Friday evening. During the week, they slept in blankets on the dirt with a tarp overhead, eating mostly pasta and beans, to finish the job. But it was a job, and it brought in a little money for the family.

Meanwhile, Margherita did what she had to do to fend for her family. She was a midwife and a mail carrier. She would also pick mushrooms in the forest and sell them to locals. Anything to ensure their survival in the poverty-stricken times that now consumed them after the war.

When I first visited San Donato in 1979 with Pina, then my girlfriend, I was shown an indentation at her eldest sister Clara's house where a soldier's bullet had grazed. They kept this as a reminder of how they had gotten through that horrific time, and how grateful they were to have made it. Unfortunately, a subsequent earthquake damaged the town severely, and Clara's house had to be rebuilt with no way to retain that deeply meaningful piece of family lore.

In 2013, the town was given a plaque by the federal government, honoring it for sheltering and saving some of its interned Jews, who were surely doomed had it not been for the *San Donatese*.

After the war, life was hard in Europe. Small towns like San Donato were as devastated as any place economically and emotionally. Ten years after the end of the war, Pina was born. Four years later, her father left, and four years after that they left behind two married siblings, Clara and Anna, as the family boarded a boat to New York. Dante had been sending money back to his family to buy food and other necessities. However, he had to borrow enough money to pay for their third-class cabin room.

Margherita and five of her brood exited through frigid New York Harbor to visit with aunts, uncles, and cousins in Flushing, Queens, before heading for Utica . . . where the streets were not "paved with gold" as was often the promise at the end of one's journey from other lands.

"My first impression of America was awe and intimidation. My relatives in Queens had tremendous amounts of food laid out on long tables with platters of meats, cheeses, tomatoes, sautéed peppers, roasted peppers, prosciutto, salami, and other Italian fare; an incomprehensible amount and variety of food that I had never experienced," Pina recalls.

She was overwhelmed by the perceived wealth of what she saw. The homes, the food, the cars, the clothes. This was certainly not what she had known in San Donato.

"The small apartment we had in Utica on Bacon Street was [bigger] than I had ever known. Despite my later realizing that we still lived in poverty in this country, at the time I didn't know that. I moved into a neighborhood in East Utica with my parents, brothers Nino and Romeo, and sisters Luciana and Marisa, where most people spoke Italian. I couldn't speak English, and it took three years, until sixth grade, when I felt that I had command of the language, and a realization that I had to work hard if I wanted to be successful in whatever field I would subsequently choose," Pina recalls.

She often sat at the living room window and gazed out at a tiny park, dreaming that she would find something better someday. Her sixth-grade teacher had spoken of her experience teaching in New Zealand before moving to Utica, a country that Pina had never heard of, but the teacher planted the seed that Pina, too, could find a way to succeed. Despite a lack of confidence, she held tightly to the notion that she had come to this country for a purpose, yet to be conceived.

"Sadly, my father and I never connected as I would have liked to. He was never truly happy in America, and his moodiness was evident in our household. My mother was at the core of our strength. She continued to work as she had in San Donato, but this was at a cheese factory where she stood on her feet for hours, being part of the assembly process. Mamma was exhausted, so we sisters would help her cook and clean. As 'the baby,' or *la citra* as it is called in our Italian dialect, she and the others seemed to want to protect me."

"You have to remember, I was born prematurely at less than four pounds, and I was the ninth of nine kids. From what I am told, it was a traumatic birth, with the perils of being born a month too soon with no neonatal care in that medieval Italian town. I was swaddled up like a doll for several months, and the prayers were uttered on a regular basis for my health. Hence, *la citra* came into this world," says Pina.

The perseverance that often takes hold of those who immigrate to create a better life for themselves became part of the fabric woven for this family, as well.

"We had a tough life, but the youngest, especially with how I came to be, was given special status. Sometimes, though, one had to fight for one's place in the family. I was always independent despite the protection afforded me by my sibling-ordered status."

"Later, only one sibling, Nino, went on the college and even earned an advanced degree. My sister Luciana went back to college as an adult. For me not only to go to college but to get a PhD was unheard of. Leave the nest? Not get married and have kids?"

"I had other plans," she says wryly.

"My family was and still is very emotional and very protective, especially of me as 'the baby.' When the three car loads of Cardarellis and extended kin took me to college, they apparently returned to Utica and hurled themselves onto my empty bed and wept uncontrollably at my leaving. (Of course I wept, too!) Still, I knew what I had to do."

Pina and I met as freshmen at State University College at Oswego in New York. I had ventured far from my Long Island roots, and she was a mere two-hour drive from her Central New York enclave. Her roommate was a friend of mine from high school, so I met her not too long after the start of school. I was struck by how beautiful and how different she was from any girl I had known in Plainview. She was studious, quiet, sweet, and just . . . different.

It was a late October Friday evening, and I had planned on visiting my friend to see if she would go to a movie and then out for a beer with me. Except she had gone to visit her boyfriend for a weekend at another state college. There was Pina studying on a Friday, and I got up the courage to ask her to go with me. Being the coward that I was, and knowing that she had a boyfriend back in Utica, I asked if she would go out with me "as friends." Of course, that was a safe request so she wouldn't know that I found her fantastically beautiful and intriguing and that normally someone like her would never go out with me. So, going "as friends" seemed safe enough, should I get rejected. Fortunately, she said yes.

Within a month we were officially dating. Within a year living together. I was even her witness when she became a citizen. Having a little hiatus from each other after graduation, but reuniting to get married in 1981, we have weathered the ebbs and flows of marriage and have been together since. Our two children, Aaron and Rebecca, marvel at the 45 years since our first date, especially because "as Mom says, she put up with you all these years!" The truth is, I am still in awe of her, and she is still my beautiful Pina. We have a strength in our relationship that seems to know no bounds. I am a lucky man.

Back in Pina's college years, one of her biology professors encouraged her to pursue science. She graduated with a degree in biology, and we moved to Albany, New York, where she worked as a lab technician at Albany Medical College. She applied for a PhD three years later but was told she'd have to prove herself in their master's program, which she did, and then could enter the PhD program; she got her doctorate in 1985.

Her perseverance to this day is evident. She went on to work in biotech and pharmaceutical companies and has been a leader in discoveries that have led to oncology medications.

"Coming from San Donato, and moving to Utica, being economically quite disadvantaged, and despite insecurities that are ever-present, I have always had the drive to succeed in a way that I knew I wanted to touch peoples' lives through research. I had to overcome a language barrier, and got teased early on before I could speak English. I strived in middle and high school because I knew that [education] was my way out, and a little over ten years after arriving in this country I was on my way to Oswego, never to look back. In fact, moving to California where we have lived for the past 33 years is a testimony to the spirit that my parents and [my sister] Mirella had when they came to America. But I have also been fortunate to have family at the center of my life. My siblings and their families are my rock, and you and the kids are my soul," Pina says.

And this country allowed a little girl from San Donato Val di Comino to find her potential, and for that she is ever grateful.

Acknowledgements

This project likely began years ago before I knew it was to be a book. Little is known about my own family of origin other than the pogroms of Eastern Europe forced my grandparents to find their way through Ellis Island to America; Brooklyn and the Bronx in New York to be precise.

The story that always captured my attention was that of my wife, Pina and her family. Their story is contained within, but it is from Pina that I learned first-hand what her family was seeking by coming to the U.S.

First and foremost I would like to thank Pina for sharing her life with me, and bringing up our children, Aaron and Rebecca, with the ethos that only one who has lived with the inner strength that is inherent in those who know where they came from, and who strive to make others' lives richer because of it. I am deeply in love with her, and indebted to her for so much.

I would also like to thank my editor, Julia Zafferano for making me sound more coherent than I did when I would send her the original drafts. Her guidance helped to shape the voices you hear as you read their stories.

Special thanks to Glenn Cantor for the photographs on the back cover.

I would like to thank family and friends for encouraging me to endeavor in this project, which truly was a labor steeped in compassion for those who have dared to accept the challenges of leaving what they have known to seek what they could only imagine. Their journeys must serve as an inspiration to always be mindful of what we offer in America, as we wrestle with how we will absorb them into this great country.

It is most important for me to acknowledge the people who came forward to be interviewed for this book. Their stories of survival needed to be told, as many of my interviewees wanted me to know. And so, it is to them, and the many refugees and immigrants who are honest and hard working, and who just want a chance to live freely in this country, this book is dedicated.

About the Author

Jordan Sher is a former social worker, where he did extensive work helping consumers with disabilities, and their families. He is also a retired middle school english and social studies teacher. Jordan was given an innovation award from the San Mateo (CA) School Boards Association for his work in bully prevention. His passion for this book was fueled after many years of both working with, and teaching adults and children from immigrant families. He holds a bachelor's degree in social sciences from SUNY Oswego (NY) and a masters in social work from SUNY Albany (NY). He lives in San Carlos, California with his wife, and has two wonderful adult children. This is his first book.

CPSIA information can be obtained
at www.ICGtesting.com
Printed in the USA
LVHW030644300821
696398LV00011B/1134